VINCENT GUERRA
THE TURNING POINT

THE WARNER PRESS
ANDERSON   INDIANA

Printed in the United States of America

For
my son Jackie
and his
generation

My special thanks to
Mrs. Imy Vrooman and my wife Ruth
for their invaluable assistance
in typing the manuscript
for this book.

CONTENTS

Chapter   *Page*

Foreword 7

1. A Liberal Education 9

2. Nightmare Begins with "H" 20

3. Hooked—But Good 40

4. A New Kind of High 56

5. A Long Way to Grow 70

6. Lightning Strikes Twice 82

7. Street Meetings and College 88

8. Marriage and Ministry 102

9. And Jackie Makes Three 115

10. Divine Appointment 120

11. A New Ministry 129

12. The Turning Point 137

Foreword

In recent months I have heard hundreds of stories like Vincent Guerra's early life, which he describes in *The Turning Point*. Stories of young lives broken and tortured and consumed by the drug parasite. I have traveled across the country talking and listening, trying to help find workable solutions to this dread malignancy.

One of the best avenues, I feel, for promoting understanding and insight into exactly what it is like to be a victim of drug addiction is first person testimonies like Mr. Guerra's. These are not pretty stories and some of them do not end well at all. Some of them describe backgrounds and influences that we can recognize in cases close to us. Some of them are so bizarre it is easy for us to shrug them off as "no wonder it happened," cases. But there are always insidious similarities and each true life story brings home again and again the magnitude and the destructive quality of drug addiction.

Important as it is to understand "why" our young people are taking the drug path and "how" the course of a young life runs once the demon has entered the bloodstream, the paramount thing we have to determine is how we can prevent it from starting and how we can stop it after it has started. These are the really tough problems.

In searching for answers, it is becoming more and more apparent that the spiritual quality of each individual life is the key guiding factor. It stands forth among young people who identify with Christ in a very personal way and know that they are loved by Him. These emotionally "secure" individuals have a special mission here on earth—to make known to others that there *is* a different kind of "high" that is very real and lasting, one that does not need to be sustained by an artificial stimulus.

After a very long, hard struggle Mr. Guerra found his way to the truth of this philosophy and we hope that as young people read his story, and others like it, they will seek help and will be able to find their own way to "The Turning Point."

ART LINKLETTER

1

A Liberal Education

When I was a year old, my father and mother broke up their marriage. Life was hard and money was scarce. Living in a cold water flat in Brooklyn, New York, we found it was difficult to sleep or keep warm without enough fuel for the stove. Sometimes when my sister and I were small, mother didn't have kerosene for the heating stove. So she would take Rose Marie and me to the train station and ride the subways all through the night. She would sit near the heater so we could all keep warm.

My mother went back to live with her father in Queens, New York. It was a disgrace in that neighborhood for a young Italian girl to be separated from her husband. The strong traditional pattern was, no matter how bad a husband might be, or how often his beatings, a wife ought to stick with him, so my mother received some persecution from different neighbors in the area.

We lived with my grandfather in a relatively happy home, although I did miss my father. My grandfather was a good provider, a carpenter by trade. He also was an excellent cook. His favorite hobby was to prepare big meals on Sunday, and there were times when my aunts and uncles came to grandfather's house. Sometimes eighteen people crowded around the table eating spaghetti and other Italian delicacies.

The day my mother enrolled me in school, I kicked up a fuss and cried for about three hours. Of course, I finally got used to school and I was a good student when a little child. I learned rapidly and grasped subjects fairly easily at first.

Then one evening my mother planned to go out with a friend of hers. Grandfather, who was drinking Italian wine, saw my mother getting dressed to go out. He became abusive, thinking mother hadn't prepared dinner for Rose Marie and me. Mother started to cry. I loved my grandfather, but not wanting him to hit my mother, I jumped on him and started pulling his hair.

I was seven years old at the time but something happened to me that night. I lost interest in school; learning didn't come easily to me anymore. After this incident between my grandfather and me, my mother even noticed that my handwriting had changed. I had had very neat penmanship but after this incident it was scrawled and carelessly done.

From the age of nine I began to connive and scheme ways to play hooky and stay away from school as much as possible. I began to despise people around me. I didn't trust anyone. I started to lie and cheat.

Finally mother moved out of my grandfather's house and into a small apartment of her own. We lived there in two and one-half rooms, my mother, sister, and I all sleeping in the one bedroom. There was no privacy for any of us. This was depressing because I had seen some of the houses my buddies lived in. Almost all my friends had their own rooms.

To escape from this gnawing feeling of nothingness, I became interested in sports. At the age of ten I did nothing but think, dream, and play baseball. When I was thirteen years old I had an opportunity to play in Yankee Stadium with the Knights of Columbus baseball team. I also had become an habitual truant. I hated school, books, and teachers. My mind was filled with resentment for everybody.

In the afternoons when I stayed home from school, almost always someone else played hooky with me. We'd buy a pack of cigarettes and go off to a place we called Baby Woods, a remote place in the center of Flushing Meadow Park. There we would hide and smoke one cigarette after another. When three o'clock came we would go home. I did this day after day.

11

Because of my playing hooky, I missed out on basic fundamentals of learning and this hindered me when I went from grade school into junior high school. Since I missed phonics, I couldn't pronounce words properly, and I missed the basics of mathematics and, therefore, became a very poor student.

In junior high school I had a teacher named Mrs. Lifer. I hated her. She was domineering and thought nothing at all of embarrassing a student in front of the whole class. She had a bad reputation among the students and I developed such hatred for her I decided to break all the windows in her classroom. One night eleven of us bombarded the school with rocks, breaking about one hundred windows.

The next day when Mrs. Lifer came into the classroom, I watched her face when she saw glass all over the floor. Her face seemed to sag. Then I told her I had helped throw the rocks. When she asked me why I did it, I told her I hated her. She broke down and began to cry. I was happy to see her cry because it showed me she wasn't as tough as she pretended to be. Her crying destroyed her image with the rest of the class and the whole school.

As a kid I liked to go to the Saturday movie. My favorite kind was war pictures. I remember one Saturday afternoon when all my friends and I saw a picture entitled *The Amboy Dukes*. This picture portrayed life in the Brownsville section of Brooklyn and areas I knew very well. It told the story of a gang of boys who called themselves the Amboy Dukes. It showed how these guys hung out on street corners and the arsenal they had. All of them carried switchblade knives and wore thick leather Garrison belts. They had a club room and some smoked marijuana. They were riotous in school and very active in gang wars. Some of the Dukes even did favors for racketeers in their neighborhood.

Soon after this movie was shown, a number of gangs formed in our area. All over New York gangs popped up overnight and gang wars were fought every day. Newspaper headlines screamed about which gang had a war, who was shot, who was arrested.

In my area a group of guys got together and called themselves the Dukes. They were a pretty rugged bunch of guys. Since I wasn't old enough to be a member of the Senior Dukes, I joined the Junior Dukes. We were about twenty-five strong. Of course we followed the pattern set by our senior club.

One of the first gang wars we fought was after a football game. Our local football team, the Rebels, played a team from Astoria. In a previous game the Astoria team had captured our Rebel flag and burned it. So, since they were playing in our territory, our Dukes wanted to get revenge. They went over to the Astoria Panther line, grabbed the flag and burned it. After the game there must have been two hundred to two hundred and fifty guys on the Duke side and about two hundred guys on the Astoria Panther side, all yelling and calling each other names.

Finally a couple of the Dukes ran over to the Panthers and started fighting and then things really broke loose. Guys were knifed, punched, kicked, stamped on, and the blood really gushed. Some of the Panthers tried to run away so the Dukes ran after them, turning over their cars. As I ran along with the big guys I suddenly met one of the Panthers. A lump jumped up in my throat, but then I saw he was more frightened than I, so I jumped into him, throwing punches at him. I kicked him with my heavy motorcycle boots.

As I kicked him I saw some boys from my junior club staring at me as if amazed that I was fighting. The big guys had told us before the fight they didn't want us involved since they didn't want us to get hurt. Because my gang saw me beat up this guy, I gained somewhat of a reputation in our neighborhood. For about a week, talk was on nothing but the gang war. This really puffed up our egos.

The junior high school I attended became a factory where we made weapons to use in gang wars. Most of the boys wore three or four heavy rings. Some made bats—we called them skaboots. We'd seen such weapons used in medieval period movies. It had a handle with a chain attached to it and on the end of the chain was a ball with spikes and rivets driven through. When we fought we swung this weapon to hit people over the head. An army .45, stolen from one of the local army bases, was given to me. This was my weapon, although I never used it in a gang war. Also, we made zip guns in school. A kid was almost forced to belong to a gang. If he didn't he was picked on by gangs in the community until, for defense, he eventually joined a gang.

There were several girl gangs in our neighborhood, some called the Debs, Furies, Cherokees. When these girls went at it they fought almost as viciously as the guys did, and they used a horrifying variety of weapons: broken bottles, pointed scissors, razor blades. Very early I formed a low opinion of girls. I began to abuse girls and had little respect for them.

By the time I was fourteen, school was just a place to go when I had nothing else to do. As a matter of fact when I did go to school, the teacher would write me a thank-you note!

In our gang wars a lot of members were injured. Some were killed. A couple of boys in my neighborhood were shot, another boy was beaten severely. One boy, while fighting in a gang war, was punched over the heart. Two days later he died from a heart attack.

Things got bad in our neighborhood. A lot of guys were sent to jail, and so many were badly hurt in fights that I was fed up at the age of seventeen. I thought to myself, if I'm going to fight and be killed,

I might as well go into the service. I couldn't hold a job, so I knew I wasn't doing anything worthwhile. I turned to the Marine Corps because some of my friends had been in the Corps. They told me how great it was, about the spirit of unity among the Marines. Once sold, I went to the recruiting office and enlisted in the Marines. I took the exam three times before I finally passed it. I even cheated the third time in order to make it. After we were sworn in, other guys told us we had made a grave mistake. But I figured that since I would be drafted eventually, I might as well go in now and get it over with.

Upon arriving at Parris Island for boot training, I found the harassing started immediately. I just about went into a state of shock—which was what I was supposed to do, I learned later. I saw kids being abused pretty badly, shaken up, some even kicked and punched. I thought, if this is the Marine Corps, I want nothing to do with it. Right away I started to hate what I was doing and my thirteen weeks at Parris Island did not change my attitude toward the Marines. I realized that the military required discipline, but felt there was room for humaneness, too.

One reason I joined the Marine Corps was to find a meaning and purpose for living I hadn't had before. My only ambition had been to become part of the Mafia, perhaps as a racketeer or a button man—a hired killer for organized crime. Since I had a very difficult time reading and spelling I thought the military might help me become better educated. What I did learn was how to march, what a rifle was for, how to fire it, and how to use skills in warfare.

After my discharge from the Marine Corps I went back to my old neighborhood, but a lot of things had changed since I left. The guys weren't fighting as much anymore and a new element—marijuana—had come into the neighborhood. When I first heard that my friends smoked pot I became annoyed. It was the philosophy in our neighborhood that Italians could smuggle the stuff in and sell it, but should never use it. We thought the only people who used it were those of other nationalities, not Italians. We felt we had more dignity than that.

When I learned my friends were smoking pot, I broke away for a little while. I was afraid to use marijuana. I became a loner, but I thought to myself one day, I might as well go back to the club and hang out with the guys. I don't have to smoke marijuana and get high. I can just stick with good wine and have fun with the chicks and all that.

One evening while I was in our storefront clubroom that we rented, two guys came in with marijuana, emptied it on the table, and rolled their own cigarettes. I was curious to see what it looked like since I had never seen marijuana before. Surprisingly, it looked like chopped parsley, catnip, or oregano. A friend of mine said, "Vinnie, why don't you try it?"

I said, "No thanks. It's not for me."

"Look, man, I've been smoking pot for a year and a half and I'm not hooked to it—I'm not a junkie. I'm not physically addicted, so why don't you try it? It's better than drinking that wine and getting sick."

I knew, of course, that when people get drunk on wine or any kind of liquor they have aftereffects. This guy was telling me that with marijuana there are no aftereffects. He said, "The only thing that happens when you come down from a marijuana high is you either eat an awful lot, or go to sleep, or both. And also there is somewhat of a depression you go through."

I asked my friend if he was lying to me about becoming a junkie and not being hooked on it. At that time authorities were saying that if you became a marijuana smoker, you would become hooked on the stuff. He insisted he was not a junkie so I said, "Okay, I'll try it." There were about nine or ten guys in the clubroom that night and when I said I'd try it, it seemed that all the guys there crowded with me into the little washroom we had.

The room was only about three feet wide and six feet long and all of us piled into the room and started smoking, all at one time. Before long the room was murky with smoke and reeked with the odor of pot. My friends were really dragging on their cigarettes. Holding their breath, they pushed the smoke up to their brains by pinching shut their noses and blowing out. They went through all sorts of contortions. I held the cigarette like it was a regular one, but my friend proceeded to show me how to smoke pot. I smoked one cigarette and didn't feel anything, so I smoked another, and another. By the fourth one I started to feel the effects of marijuana.

After I got high, I walked into the clubroom which had indirect lighting and colored lights. I really started to groove on the lights. The colors seemed more intense and I had the feeling of floating. A couple of my friends put on some rock-and-roll records and I really dug the sounds. The beat seemed more intense and profound. The guys started dancing by themselves, moving in time with the music. After about an hour of talking, laughing, and sometimes hysterics, one fellow suggested we go to the Three Star, a bar we hung out in when not in the clubroom.

After we arrived there, my friend Bobby came over to me and said, "Man, wait till you taste beer when you're high on pot. The taste is like something else!" Many of the boys started drinking Coke, since the sweet taste was exaggerated. We started to rap with some of the people in the Three Star, make fun of them and laugh at the customers.

One guy in particular, a little fellow named Jimmy, sounded like a girl when he talked. We started laughing and poking fun at him. This was the effect smoking pot had on us. Of course, the "in" thing to do when on grass was to put on a pair of sunglasses. Wearing them was psychologically lifting, and it seemed the high was increased by wearing them. It also was considered "cool" to wear dark shades.

When under the influence of pot, I—and many of my friends also—experienced a time-and-space distortion. For instance, many nights we drove automobiles while under the influence of pot. Sometimes it seemed we were barreling ninety miles an hour when we would only be creeping about ten or twenty miles an hour. Other times, when we were hitting ninety miles an hour it seemed we were crawling only ten miles an hour. It seemed at times to take an eternity to travel down one street, especially when it was raining and the windshield wipers were used.

We would start to groove on the windshield wipers, and the pattern of the rain on the windows would make us forget we were driving an automobile.

One night we were cruising down one of the main arteries in New York City. The boy driving was considered a very good driver. He had driven in many drag races and often won. He had tremendous reflexes, yet one night, when we were all under the influence of pot, Rusty decided to make a right-hand turn, but made it fifty yards too soon. We slammed into a parked car, injuring several of us in the car.

I learned by experience there are several types of marijuana. Some marijuana, when I got high from it, seemed to knock the socks right off my feet. I'd get so bombed out I wouldn't be able to function because it was so strong. This kind usually came from Panama. Then there is the type that comes from Mexico or Africa, and these marijuanas have different effects on different personalities.

Although marijuana isn't physically addicting, a person develops a psychological dependence upon it. Young people take acid (LSD), pot, pills, and speed to enjoy rock festivals, love-ins, private parties, or jam sessions. They are bored if they don't have drugs, because they're psychologically dependent upon these drugs in order to have a good time.

Well, I smoked marijuana for about a year and a half. One night my friends wanted to go out and try something more potent. My start on one drug—and marijuana is a drug—had lessened my fear of trying different drugs. Once I broke the ice by using pot or maybe taking an occasional pill, such as Seconal or

Tuinal (goofball), my worst fear of drugs was over. Two of my friends got some heroin, and liked it.

They came back to the clubhouse and told a couple of the other fellows how great the feeling was, like this high was really where it's at, it was the thing to do. These boys got about four other fellows to try it. Of course, these other four fellows tried it, dug it, so they in turn came back to the clubroom and told other guys about it. Before long, of the twenty guys who belonged to our little club, fifteen started to use heroin. Thirteen of those fifteen heroin users became hard-core junkies. My turn was soon to come, another step in my liberal education.

2

Nightmare Begins with "H"

I didn't start to use heroin right away. But one night I had an argument with my stepfather and mother. Depressed, I went to the hangout and when my friends noticed my despondency, one said, "Why don't you try getting high on heroin? It'll make you feel better and forget your problems."

So I said, "Okay, I'll try it." I was really looking for a way out. We went to my house, since my parents were away for the weekend. The boys took out their heroin and prepared to sniff it. They emptied the contents of the heroin bags onto a small mirror and chopped it into fine granules. Then they made little matchbook-cover shovels, scooped the dust into them, and sniffed the heroin.

One of my friends came over to me and said, "Okay, Vince, it's time for you to turn on." And I did. That experience started a nightmare that lasted four and one-half years. As I sniffed the heroin my nose started to burn and my eyes watered, but it was about fifteen minutes before I felt the effects of the heroin. My head felt heavy, yet light. Certain parts of my body, especially around my face and nose, started to itch. I became very light-headed and heavy in thought. I started to scratch and rub my nose in a slow-motion way, but with vigor, and I became care-free. I didn't care about anyone around me or anything at all, although I felt sick in my stomach.

As we were leaving my house, working our way toward the car, the drug started to work even more on me, so I lit a cigarette. I retched, yet the feeling was a good feeling. Sitting in the car, I began to nod, closed my eyes, and drifted into a little Utopia. I've known drug users to nod while smoking cigarettes, sometimes catching their clothes on fire. Sometimes the cigarette burned down to their fingertips. At times the person is so drugged the cigarette burns right between his fingers and he knows nothing about it until the next day when the drug has worn off.

I always told myself I would use drugs only on weekends, but as far as my becoming a junkie, or a dope fiend, it would never happen to me—I thought. At first, I used heroin just on weekends, only three dollars a weekend, and I was able to keep my job. Then my body started to build up a tolerance and my mind craved the drug since it was a good way to escape. From three dollars a weekend, the cost rose to three dollars every two days, then three dollars a day.

One day a group of guys were up in my friend's bedroom. We didn't have enough heroin to go around. One of the guys showed us a set of works, a home-made hypodermic needle. So instead of sniffing this time, a couple of the fellows main-lined, that is they drove the needle into the large vein in their arm and shot up. A number of us did that and the rush, or jolt, was something of a new experience for us.

Before long three-dollar bags weren't potent enough. We had to go to five-dollar bags, then fifteen-dollar bags, then twenty-dollar bags, and on and on. I'd shoot as much heroin as I could get my hands on and it finally got to the point where I was no longer using heroin, but heroin was using me. I realized, after using heroin for about three months, that I had a habit.

I woke up one morning with wrenching pains in my back, cramps in my legs, and loose bowels, so I went to a friend of mine and told him what I was experiencing. He only laughed at me and said, "You have a chippy," which is a mild habit. I knew one thing: I was sick, nauseous; I had a hollow feeling in the pit of my stomach; beads of sweat ran down my face, yet I felt cold.

Seeking relief, I went home, took one of my $100 suits and sold it at a pawn shop. I was fast reaching the point where I was living from fix to fix. I had a pretty good job in a clothing store warehouse in Long Island, but I soon lost it. I couldn't keep a job anywhere and I had to leave home because of too many conflicts in the family. I felt looked down upon as a disgrace to the community and to society. But I'd developed the attitude: They're all squares who don't know where it's at; so who cares what they think anyway! I thought even my friends who didn't turn to heroin were squares.

The hardest thing for me to face up to when I was a junkie was the fact that my family rejected me. This hurt more than anything else because at one time my uncles and aunts and I were very close. But now they disowned my cousin and me. My cousin Jackie, also a drug user, and I went to live with my sister, Rose Marie. We couldn't stay in our own homes, so the only person who would take us in was Rose Marie. At Thanksgiving time our mothers tried to get permission for us to sit at the table for Thanksgiving dinner, but the men said no.

My mother and aunt gave us some money to go to the movies, so we went out, bought some heroin, shot up, and then sneaked into the theater. Even though high on drugs, I sat in that movie house, looked around, and asked myself, "What's going to become of me?" The only other person in the theater that day was an old derelict and I thought, That's me in about another ten years. I got scared because I really didn't want that to happen to me.

After the movie, we decided to go back to my sister's apartment right above Jackie's home. Since my uncle didn't know we were staying up there, we had to sneak in. We were hungry so my aunt and mother went downstairs to bring us some food. When my uncle and my stepfather found out the food was for us, they said we couldn't have anything. Food had to be smuggled to us in a garbage pail.

The approach in our neighborhood concerning curing a drug addict was to either beat the drugs out of the user, throw him down into the cellar or chain him to a radiator for five or six days. With nothing but bread and water for nourishment, this was supposed to cure the addict. When a person uses drugs for an extended period of time, as Jackie and I did, something happens to him. He becomes a sick person in the sense that he's not responsible for what he's doing when addicted to the drug. What he needs is compassion and understanding and professional treatment by those who know what they're doing—who know how to communicate with drug users.

Some friends of mine were literally chained to their beds and kept on leashes like dogs. Their fathers would say, "If you want to live like a dog, you're going to be treated like a dog!" One put a collar on his son's neck and, when the guy wanted to go out, his father took him out on a leash and walked him like a dog. Of course, this treatment only turned the kids off. As soon as they were free they ran away from home and went right back on drugs.

My real father got word that I was using drugs. He was the type who punched first and asked questions later, though he and I had a pretty good relationship whenever we saw each other. We seemed to have a good time together, going into bars and drinking.

After I started using drugs and became hooked, I didn't do much drinking. Like most addicts, I transferred my dependence from alcohol to drugs. My father sent for me, saying he wanted to talk to me. I knew this meant he probably would use a baseball bat on me, or something else.

I put my stiletto in my coat pocket and went to one of the bars in Brooklyn where dad was waiting for me. When I first walked into the darkened tavern, I saw no one except the bartender. Then, becoming accustomed to the dimness, I saw my father sitting way at the back in one of the booths. When I looked him straight in the eye, I felt that something was going to break. The place was as quiet as a jungle before a storm strikes. I put my hand on the knife—I had decided that if he laid one hand on me I was going to stick him. I knew it was wrong, but I was going to kill my father or stab him if he touched me.

He asked if I was using drugs and I said no, I wasn't. He said, "I've heard that drug addicts don't drink."

I said, "That's true."

"Then how about having a drink." And he bought some liquor which I forced down. He asked me if I would roll up my sleeves and show him my arms. Before going to meet him I had shaved my arms and put cocoa butter on them, hoping this would hide the tracks, or needle marks. I did this because I figured he would ask to see my arms. I pulled up my sleeves and when he couldn't see any marks, he said, "So what's all the story about you using narcotics?"

I told him, "I don't know. There are a lot of guys in my neighborhood who use junk. So I guess I have the name too." He believed me and seemed to think there was nothing to it. This made me happy since I didn't want to hurt my own father. Before I left him we talked about my future. I was out of work, and he knew it. He wanted me to get a job and get married.

I made sure I got a few dollars from him so I could go out and get some dope. I then hurried back to my neighborhood, got a couple of the fellows, went out and bought some drugs, and shot up. I learned to do some pretty unscrupulous things to get enough narcotics to maintain my drug habit. But scruples mean little to drug addicts.

I've known nice girls, some from decent homes, some from the ghettos, who became prostitutes, selling their bodies for a three-dollar or five-dollar bag of heroin. Some parents sent their children out to get money for them so they could buy drugs. Some young guys were forced to become male prostitutes. Some people seemed willing to take advantage of young people and the predicaments they were in, to use them for their own lustful ways. Then, when they finished using them, they wadded them up like a scrap of paper and threw them off to the side. There they rotted, like vegetables, with no morals or sense of values or motivation to do anything.

When these young people did try to go straight, their minds were so corrupted and distorted that the chances of their going straight were practically nil. Some of these drug abusers tried to go straight, but they couldn't look their parents in the face so great were their guilt feelings. In turn, they only became more involved in the drug world and corruption around them.

When a kid in this type of environment begins to sink, he starts to grab onto things, usually drugs. He uses them more and more since drugs seem to numb the pain and unpleasant memories. Such was my case. I felt as though walls were closing in all around me and I needed something to sustain me, since I wasn't strong enough to do it on my own. I, too, began to go under in the flood of confusion and fear, so I resorted to drugs to give me a false sense of security. When I was in the utopia provided by narcotics, nothing seemed to matter.

Some young kids I knew turned to drugs to dampen the shock of seeing a parent in bed with persons other than the rightful spouse. When I was still on drugs, I asked one fourteen-year-old boy why he was using drugs. He said, "Well, my mother's a pig. She's no good. And what's in life for me anyway? Nobody cares about me." As a result, he became a junkie.

The life of a junkie is a hustle. He goes to bed at night thinking about one thing: the fix in the morning. When he wakes in the morning, if he doesn't have a supply, he has to get dressed quickly, go out and pull a fast score before he gets too sick to get around.

The routine for my cousin and me was to get up early in the morning, get dressed and go to someone's house or someplace where there was money; then we'd steal, connive, scheme in order to get it. Most of the time, after we got our morning shot, we'd go to department stores in the afternoon.

Our favorite place to steal from was a large department store in Long Island. We stole quite a bit of merchandise: mink coats, cashmere coats, things that would sell easily. We estimated that the amount of money we spent in six months came to about ten thousand dollars which wasn't very much compared to some people. Some guys went through eighty thousand dollars a year. Nevertheless it's an awful lot of money to raise by boosting—shoplifting. We'd steal an item that cost perhaps two hundred dollars and take it to either a pusher or a fence, one who buys stolen merchandise. For it we would be given maybe ten or fifteen dollars for a two hundred dollar article. This is what we had to do every day to get money for drugs. Many of us also became dope pushers.

We used to hang out in a bar in Corona in Queens. It was a sharp, groovy, little place, dark inside. And it had a good jazz combo. Many nights we'd go up there with our girls and just dig the sounds. But one night we noticed an altogether different clientele. There was a big dance floor in the back, behind a partition which divided the dance floor from the bar area. As my friends and I walked in we felt as if we were in a strange place, everything looked so different. We asked the proprietor, "What's going on around here?"

He said, "Certain people have taken over the place. They're going to lease the bar out." As we looked around we noticed the guys at the bar were acting very strange, very feminine. Then one guy came over to me and started eyeing me up and down. He told me that I was cute. I told him if he came near me I'd punch his teeth out. He just made a big joke out of it and said, "My, my, isn't he tough!" and the other guys at the bar began to laugh.

I looked at my friends and said, "Let's clean house and get these fagots out of our bar!"

The proprietor, seeing what had happened, came over and calmed us down, buying us a couple of drinks. The neighborhood cop, who was everybody's friend because he knew what was going on but didn't do anything about it, came over and said we'd be able to make a lot of money with this place in the neighborhood. We didn't know what he was talking about. There were four men who owned this place now and one of them came over to me and said, "How'd you like to see what's going on in the back room?"

I said, "The back room? What for?"

He took me behind the partition to the dance floor. When we walked in the back I saw these guys dancing with each other, and girls dancing with each other. When I saw this I just about blew my mind! I'd never seen anything like this before in my life. These guys were dancing and kissing each other and it turned my stomach. Then I saw these beautiful looking girls dancing with other girls and they were doing the same thing. I looked at the man and said, "What have you done? Man, this is a freaky place!"

He just laughed at me and said, "Well, that's just the way these people are. There's a lot of money in it." So this man, Dave, took me aside and said, "How would you like to work for me?"

I asked, "Why me?"

"Well, you look like you can handle yourself."

"What do you want me to be here, a bouncer? I'm not about to bounce anybody out of here! Most of my friends would come here and I'm not about to bounce them out of the place."

He said, "No, if that's the case then you'll have a job and you won't even have to work, but you'll be getting paid for it." He asked me if I was working and I told him that I was making one hundred and twenty-five dollars a week, but I wasn't. I was out of a job. He said, "Well, I'll match that salary and you'll have to work only three nights a week."

I said okay and talked it over with my friends. They felt it was a pretty good thing for me to get into. These people didn't know I was a junkie, so I had $125 coming in every week and I wasn't doing anything except keeping an eye on the joint. If the police came in I would hit the button which lit up the whole back room, indicating that the Man was on the premises. The groups would change partners, boys dancing with girls. So when the officers came in they didn't catch them dancing with each other.

I saw some pretty weird things happen at this place. One time two guys became engaged. Men already married would go there and have a male lover waiting for them. All of this bothered me, but the money was coming in.

While I was working at this lounge, the place was really rocking one night. A lot of kids came in from a televised disc jockey show. Most of the guys who came in walked like girls. I noticed a tall, blonde-haired girl in the bar area who was really mouthing off. I started to laugh at some of the things she did. She swore so strongly I went over and started making small conversation with her, asking where she was from, who she was with.

Later, a friend of mine came over to me and said, "That chick you were just talking to is a prostitute."

I couldn't believe it because she was so clean-cut looking—dirty talking but clean looking. He told me she made a lot of money. He said I ought to latch on to her because then more money would be coming into my pocket. So I started talking with her and we did a little bit of drinking. This started a friendship that lasted about six months.

This girl was also a drug user. She told me that as long as I didn't become an alcoholic she could take my being hooked, but as soon as I started to booze it, our friendship would end. Her father, she said, was an alcoholic who used to come home at night and beat her and her mother. Soon she wanted to use drugs more, but I told her not to because she'd become a junkie and once that happened she wouldn't appeal to men anymore and she couldn't make any money. She wanted to use more, she said, because when she was on drugs it made her job as a prostitute easier.

She said she was over twenty-one and could do as she pleased, so she started to use junk quite heavily. As a result she became hooked. Two wrongs, I figured, didn't make a right and I decided to break away from her. I was hooked on heroin pretty badly, so I decided to go to Florida and kick my habit.

With sixty dollars in my pocket, I went to a hotel in Florida where I laid up for four days, off drugs and violently sick. My mother called me, since she was interested in knowing what I was doing and where I was. I told her I was kicking my habit, that I was sick of using drugs and wanted to stop and make a new life for myself. Mother sent me twenty-five dollars so I could stay there longer.

After the fifth day I started to really enjoy myself and did a lot of swimming and lying around in the sun. It was the first time I'd ever been to Florida and while there I met a couple of boys who provided me some pot and pills. After ten or eleven days in Florida I went back to New York City looking healthy and heavily tanned.

The girl I'd left was quite glad to see me, and the first thing I asked her was for some junk. Of course, she was only too willing to give me some. She gave me a bag of heroin and I shot up, which started me using drugs all over again. I was making two hundred and twenty-five dollars a week plus getting money from another girl I was going with at the time. I was making about five hundred dollars a week in all, and at the end of each week I hoped I would have something to show for it because I had always wanted to start a bank account. But at the end of the week I had nothing to show but more needle marks on my arms.

Well, a guy has to do some pretty fast hustling in New York to make a few bucks to keep him going. When a junkie tries to buy drugs, he sometimes has pretty weird experiences. A guy might go alone to buy five or six bags of heroin. Two junkies might spot him in the neighborhood, so after the guy makes the buy, the two junkies will jump him and take his dope away. This is what we called a "rip-off."

Nor can you be sure just when the Man is going to jump on you. We were stopped several times by narcotics agents, but I'll never forget one time when we went down to East Twentieth Street and Tenth Avenue in downtown New York. At that time it was very hard to get drugs because a panic had hit the city. During a panic very little heroin is sold on the street corners because of the heat from narcotics officers. We made a fast connection and the guy we bought from told us to split because the Man was behind us.

Although we burned rubber getting away from the corner, the police cruiser squealed after us. I made a left turn but the officer made the same turn. After several turns and still being followed, I decided to really gun it. We were in Chinatown, in downtown Manhattan where the streets are wide enough for only one car to travel.

I stepped on it, hitting sixty-five miles an hour down those narrow streets, but the cruiser gained on us. I ran through red lights, stop signs—it was a miracle we weren't in an accident. Each time I'd just beat a light the officer would be stopped by it. So he'd give a blast on his siren and the traffic would let him through. Well, I came to a corner and two guys in different cars formed a wedge so I couldn't get through. When I saw what the two cars had done I yelled to my friends, "Throw the junk out the window." Hoping the policeman wouldn't see it, we screeched to a stop.

The policeman jumped out of his car, pulled his gun, and stalked over to the driver's side of our car. Putting my hands over my stomach, I pretended to be sick. Rubbing my eyes to make them water I told the officer I was hurrying to St. Vincent Hospital in downtown New York. He asked for the car's registration. Luckily we had it with us.

I forgot that I had a ten-dollar bag of marijuana in my back pocket and when the cop grabbed me by the seat of my pants his hand went right over the marijuana. The drug was wrapped in a Kleenex which he jerked out and held in his hand, not knowing there was something in it. He searched us, then ordered us to wait while he called the Motor Vehicle Bureau to check on the car to see if it was stolen.

After he hung up, the cop came over to us and said, "Lucky for you guys I just got a more important call. Otherwise I'd run you in and charge you all!" He told us to split, to get lost. When he was out of sight we went around the corner to find the dope we had thrown from the car. We got it, went home, and shot up.

These things happened time and time again. Also, you could always expect to be cheated. Sometimes when buying junk from a dope pusher we didn't know too well, we might be sold baking soda or milk sugar. You never knew because the junkie world is a very plastic world, a phony world.

People we thought we could trust often let us down. I never knew when I was going to be arrested. Or when I was going to take that last shot in my arm. I never knew what would happen from day to day.

At this time, too, the lounge where I was still working began to be raided frequently. The boss thought it would be wise to close down before someone was arrested. The vice squad often came in and the narcotics agents were usually there checking. Strangely, they never seemed to know I was using drugs. The owners told me if I kept my nose clean and did the right thing, they would put me in complete charge of the next bar they opened. It would be mine.

Because of my using drugs, though, I really didn't care to become a bar owner or even a button man anymore. I knew I'd had it. I couldn't do that type of work anymore because I couldn't keep a secret. If I were arrested I would get sick, and in order to get a shot of heroin I would rat on somebody—tell whatever the police wanted to know. Very few junkies can keep a secret.

My sister took Jackie and me in again. We stole to maintain my drug habit, at least one hundred to one hundred-fifty dollars a day. Jackie and I were close, inseparable. I'd turn him on if I had drugs and he'd turn me on if he had some, so we relied on each other. I felt he was the only person I could trust and he felt the same about me, though often when we were both using drugs we had loud arguments, but never came to blows.

One night I was really uptight and sick because I needed a fix badly. I loved and respected my sister probably more than anyone else. I knew Rose Marie was a decent person who really loved people. Really uptight because I didn't have any money, I thought, *Man, here I am a junkie! There probably are places where I could get a fix and not have to steal from anyone.* So I called a veteran's hospital. I thought an ex-marine could get help from them. They told me they didn't have facilities for people like me.

Then I thought, *Since I couldn't get anything from the hospital, I'll try the police department and tell them I'm a junkie who wants to kick and I need help.* When I called the police department the officer at the desk said, "We're not running a hotel here! Call back at eight o'clock tomorrow morning."

Sick and needing a fix, my last resort was to steal some money and the closest money to me was in my sister's purse, which was on her night table. She was sleeping, so I tiptoed into her bedroom, opened her pocketbook and took five dollars, leaving her fifteen cents for her bus fare to work the next morning. I walked to the main highway leading into New York City and hitchhiked a ride into the city where I bought a bag of dope. I felt very sick because I had stolen money from my sister—I really didn't want to but I had to because I was uptight and needed a fix.

I called my sister the next day and apologized. She invited me back to her place, saying she realized I wasn't myself but was sick and needed help. When I got there, my mother, also at Rose Marie's, was very upset. Everybody got emotional and started crying and all that. They asked me if I wanted to go to a hospital. I was afraid to because at the time I had no police record, nobody knew I was a junkie, and I didn't want it on my record. So I told them no, and ran away, living in the streets, sleeping in parks and cold water flats, walking the streets at night, and, of course, stealing every day.

One time Jackie and I stole a cashmere coat. Thinking the coast was clear, I went walking out of the store with it. The store detective came up to me, stuck his gun in my ribs, and said, "Don't run away, don't move!" I told him he didn't have to worry, I wasn't planning on going anyplace. When I felt that gun in my ribs I hoped he would pull the trigger because I was so tired of running, stealing, lying. Normally weighing about 210 pounds, I was down to 160 pounds. I was glad when he said I was under arrest, glad because I really wanted to be off the streets.

They took me to the interrogation room and asked me where I lived, what was my dope, who was with me in the store, and all this. I had just taken a shot about an hour before we went out stealing so I didn't tell them anything and I didn't get sick. They handcuffed me and took me down to the Tombs in New York City where they mugged and fingerprinted me. That night when I went for an arraignment before the court the judge asked me how I pleaded. I said, "I'm guilty. I did it and now I want what's coming to me. Don't even bother notifying my parents." The judge asked me if I had a lawyer, but I said I didn't want one, so he told the court authorities to notify my parents and to get me a lawyer.

The next day they sent me over to Long Island City prison. I was coming down from my drugs and started going through cold turkey, which is withdrawing from narcotics without any medication, and man did I get sick! I was so sick I could feel every nerve in my body twitch and cry out for drugs. I went through unbelievable contortions, experiencing agonizing pain I can't put into words—vomiting, diarrhea, sniffles, watery eyes. But the worst of it all was I couldn't sleep. I kept saying, "Oh, if I could only get an hour's sleep!" But I just couldn't relax.

This lasted four and one-half days. Finally, after the fifth day, I started to come around. I chucked, which means I recovered my appetite. It got so I could hardly wait for the guard to bring the food to my cell. Too, while I was in jail I started thinking about my life and what I was going to amount to. The only thing I could see ahead for me was death or life on the skids. I recalled The Bowery in downtown New York, my mind seeing derelicts: the way they shuffled around, staggering, holes in their shoes, filthy, ragged clothes, bearded. I often thought that was just what I would end up being, a derelict. As I sat in jail, I thought about my education. I could hardly read or write. My mind kept nagging, *Wish I had a fix so I could erase all these problems.*

I decided that maybe I could get help from somebody so, thinking a clergyman would be the best person to go to, on Saturday I went to see the prison chaplain. I told him, "Sir, I'm a junkie. I've been shooting drugs for about four years but now I want out. I want a new life."

He looked at me and said, "Son, for guys like you there is very little hope." At that time the philosophy was, once a junkie, always a junkie. "Let me give you this bit of advice, though," he added. "Go to church on Sundays and obey your mother and father."

Well, I couldn't go that route because the lines of communication between my parents and me were broken. As for my going to church, well, there was nothing for me in the established church. I thought, *why go sit next to some hypocrite who plays Holy Joe on Sunday for one hour and does his thing during the rest of the week?* That wasn't my bag! I went back to my cell filled with resentment for the church and for society in general.

My cousin Jackie had been arrested about a day after I was picked up. He was released on bail but his parents remanded his bail so he was put back in jail with me. He thought I had ratted him out because we had been stealing coats together, but his mother finally told him she had remanded his bail. After spending several days in jail we went back to court for bail setting. Since Jackie had a few previous arrests and I didn't have a record, his bail was higher than mine. The only other time I had been busted was when I was thirteen and that didn't really count. After we were released, my mother took us home.

She said she was going to keep her eyes on us, she wasn't going to let us out of her sight, and all this. I knew that if I felt I had to go out and shoot drugs, I'd do it, no matter how mother would try to stop me, because the desire, the mental craving, is stronger than the physical want for heroin. So, we got home and I thought of myself as a walking dead man, no hope of ever breaking the drug habit.

The first chance I had I took ten dollars from my mother's purse and split. Jackie and I bought some drugs, shot up, and got high. Of course we had been cured physically, but there was still the mental habit. A person can be a junkie for ten years and then stop, not using the works for a great length of time. But during the time he's not using, if he still toys with the idea of getting high and jabbing the needle in his arm that person is still a junkie. Drug addiction, I found, is not only a physical state of need but also a deficiency in the user's mind.

Many times I tried to kick the habit on my own. I'd go to my aunt's house on Long Island and take cough medicine with codeine in it to ease some of the pain. But while kicking this habit I was only fooling myself. I learned to lie to myself, then believed my own lies. I'd tell myself I was going to stay off drugs, knowing full well that when I went back to the city I'd shoot up again. I was always looking for that rush, that sensation I got when I'd first put the needle in my arm. But I never got it.

Like a lot of junkies, I kept longing for that same rush I had when I first started shooting. I was arrested again, and my parents bailed me out. After the second time I was bailed out of jail, my stepfather wouldn't allow me to live in the same house my mother lived in. So again I stayed with Rose Marie.

3

Hooked–But Good

As a junkie I saw some frightening things. One night Jackie and I were going home from shooting up. We drove into Corona, parked, and sat under the marquee of a theater, which was near the overhead elevator of the Flushing subway, we called it the "El." There was a lot of racial tension in our community, and I resented blacks, Puerto Ricans, Irish. As a matter of fact, I was prejudiced against anyone who wasn't Italian.

As we sat on the curb nodding out under sedation, feeling the effects of the heroin, a group of black girls and boys walked up the street toward the subway. Seeing two white girls with them, the kids with us started casting slurs at the white girls.

The black guys spouted back and verbal insults were exchanged. Some of our guys ran after the other guys to beat them up. The blacks ran to the subway elevator, pulled their knives, and threw garbage pails at the whites. I didn't want to get involved because I was feeling too high. My friends came down yelling, "They've got knives! They've got knives."

Jackie, who had a pistol in his car, grabbed it. I went for the jack in the trunk of the car. While I was trying to get the jack unscrewed from the spare tire, I heard someone coming up behind me.

Immediately I spun around, throwing my hand over my face. I felt something like a stinging pinch. I came down hard with the part of the jack that goes under the bumper, smashing my attacker across the face. I saw the flesh split open and blood spurt out. When I looked down at the person, I realized it was a black girl. I got sick. If it had been a guy I probably wouldn't have felt too bad about it, but since it was a girl, I didn't know what to do.

41

Then a white girl started screaming. Panicking, I ran over, yanked her hair, and hit her in the face. The wail of sirens scattered my friends, so Jackie and I jumped in the car and raced for home. That night I made plans to leave the country because I thought the black girl was dead. When I'd looked at her, her eyes were rolled back in her head and she lay so still.

However, the next day I went back to the hangout and saw this same girl walking up and down the street looking for guys who were present the night before.

I looked at her, wondering if she would recognize me since I'd had my hand over my face when I hit her. She walked over to me and said I was one of the fellows who was there.

I said, "What on earth are you talking about? I was out with my girl friend last night."

"Are you sure you weren't here last night?"

I told her I wasn't there so, since she wasn't sure, she left. They did arrest a couple of my friends for what had happened, but when it came time for the trial this Negro girl didn't show up, so charges were automatically dropped.

Then there were nights when my cousin and I would go home to my sister's place, high, nodding out and smoking cigarettes. When a junkie gets high he smokes an awful lot. One time when my cousin fell asleep with a cigarette in his hand, Rose Marie's couch just about went up in flames.

Another time Jackie and I thought we'd try to kick the habit together. Jackie's mother owned a summer home out in Sound Beach, Long Island. So we told his mother we were going out there to kick the habit. She said to go ahead, that she'd be out the next day. Jackie and I rode a Long Island train, to get there. We had two bags of dope we were going to shoot, the last time we'd be high.

We got to the summer home and, since it was early spring, found it was a bit chilly. We cooked up our dope, shot up, and got high, both of us in bed. I had never before fallen asleep with a cigarette in my hand, even when I was high on drugs. But this time I did. As if in a dream, I felt little things pinching me and I'd half wake up and put out the flames, not realizing I was on fire. Before long I started to smell flesh burning. Both Jackie and I woke up and realized I was on fire. Fortunately, I was not badly burned.

Many times, when we tried to kick, our parents would buy medicine for us. One time I tried to kick on my own, so my mother and I went to see the doctor. He gave me some medication but, instead of using it properly, I used the medicine to get high. I learned to con and scheme to get drugs.

When Jackie and I were staying at Rose Marie's, we slept on her sectional couch, Jackie on one side and I on the other. One night I dreamed of Jackie in a coffin. I dreamed I saw him lying there, still, and a voice seemed to say, "In one year Jackie will die. You will die six months later." I woke up with a start because everything was so lifelike. I looked over where Jackie was sleeping to make sure he was really there and not already dead. I finally went back to sleep, then, but I dreamed about Jesus Christ nailed to the cross. As real as life, I saw the redness of dripping blood, and his body white like marble. He seemed to say, "I will watch over you." That was the end of my dream. I woke up and thought, *I must be cracking up.* I staggered to the kitchen sink, splashed cold water in my face, drank some milk, and went back to bed. I was terribly upset because of this dream.

The next day I told my cousin about it. He just laughed, so I laughed. But I think he seemed to be a bit disturbed. During that whole year we lived it up, but it was a very sad year because a number of our friends were found dead from taking overdoses.

A young fellow by the name of Philly was found dead in his own bed, the needle still in his arm. His mother discovered his body.

A young girl, Ellen, was found dead in the lobby of her apartment building. An occasional user, she went out joyriding with some boys one night and took a little too much stuff. The fellows, thinking she was just in a coma, took her to her fashionable apartment house, laid her on the sofa in the lobby, and rang her parents' doorbell. They thought her parents would come right down and find her. Unfortunately, though, her parents were out and no one came down to answer the door. When her parents came home later, they found their daughter on the sofa, dead from an overdose of narcotics.

A young man, who tried many times to quit drugs, was found dead in the bathroom of his home. He had tried religion, as such, but never had a personal encounter with Christ. I suppose he thought his just going to church and living a clean life were sufficient.

Another fellow was killed while riding his motorcycle. He drove through a barbed wire fence and his whole body was mutilated. It was a very sad year.

After Jackie and I went to court for grand larceny, the judge sentenced him to six months on Rikers Island. I was given a suspended sentence with the recommendation that I go to one of the city hospitals. I was crushed, because my cousin was getting time and I was going to the hospital. I felt he was being gypped; I looked at Jackie and we gave each other a last little nod. I gave him my cigarettes and all the money I had, and he was taken to the bullpen. As he disappeared from sight, I felt completely wiped out.

Leaving the court, I went home and called one of the city hospitals. I went to one on East Nineteenth Street, right across the street from Bellevue Hospital, to be interviewed. I had to tell how much heroin I used, how often, for how long. They said it would be about a week before I could be admitted into the hospital. I asked for drugs or medicine to keep me until I was admitted, but was told, "No, it's something you'll have to work out on your own."

I talked to my mother about it and she consented to give me money to buy heroin until I was admitted to the hospital. I really tried to cut down my habit on my own. Finally, one day, the phone rang and a hospital receptionist stated they had a bed for me. So without hesitation I went to the hospital.

My friend Dominic took me down, and before I went into the hospital he asked me for my shoes. His were full of holes. At the hospital I was given methadone to bring me down. I was put on a detoxification program. I had no personal interviews with psychiatrists, and the place was run somewhat like a jail. I couldn't leave the ward I was in. I had to stay on one floor. Most of the guys in there were prisoners who were drying out, but who were waiting to go back on the streets and use again.

They had devised ways of smuggling dope and heroin into the place, though. One of the boys had a line which reached from the fifth floor, where we were, to the pavement of the street. His friends would bring him dope, tie it to the line, and the guy in the hospital would pull it up. Many nights though, the girls on the third floor, knowing what was happening, would cut the line and take the dope.

It was hard to go straight or even think of kicking my habit in a place like that. Ninety percent of the conversation was about the highs or the experiences we'd had. It was an ego type thing and we gloried in our actions. After nineteen days in the hospital I stopped using medication. I was starting to eat well again. I thought I could make it, so I decided to leave the hospital. The day I left was also the release date for the guy I used to buy all my dope from.

This fellow and I were tight, so when we were outside the hospital he said, "Vince, I have eight bags stashed in my room. How about coming back with me and banging four up and then we'll call it quits."

I looked at him and said, "I'll see you, Ray," and turned away. I forced myself to run at top speed to the subway station. I headed for home. I had checked out of the hospital with eight dollars in my pocket. On the subway I saw one of my friends, Tony, one of the guys who hung out with us and who was also a head. Knowing I'd go back on drugs if we started talking, I ducked down so he couldn't see me.

I went to my sister's house, since I still wasn't allowed to go back home. I was certain someone would greet me when I arrived. To my dismay, there wasn't anyone home. What a letdown it was to be greeted by an empty house.

That eight dollars I had was burning a hole in my pocket and I felt the urge to buy dope. Instead I went out and got a haircut. Right next to the barber shop was an Italian restaurant. I went in and bought a big Italian dinner, blowing my eight dollars. I was broke, but it made me breathe easier. About four o'clock

I went back to my sister's and my mother was there. They seemed so glad to see me! Again, I lived with my sister for a while.

They didn't bug me at first to get a job, but after a week or so my stepfather called and asked if I wanted to work. I said yes, so he got me a job on construction and I made quite a bit of money. I still had a desire, a craving, to get high but something kept me from using the needle.

One day, on Saturday, after I had worked and hadn't used drugs for about a month, I went to a place called Forest Hills where I saw my friend Dominic with his girl. They both were high, so I broke over, bought heroin, and shot up. While working on construction I made about one hundred and seventy-five dollars a week, so I tried to stay away from drugs, even though I used that one time. I started drinking heavily, though, spending about eighty dollars a weekend on hard liquor and Scotch.

47

After coming home from work I never wanted to go out, because I was so tired and my hands were all cut up from the rough steel I handled. I began to shape up physically and my stepfather, at whose side I worked, made sure I worked hard so I'd want to go home and sleep. He kept me busy and I soon became almost as efficient and skilled as he. Gradually though, I drank more and more.

Most of the neighborhood kids hung out in the bowling alley so I went there to see what it was like. I met the bartender, Dominic, from my old neighborhood. Dominic and I got along real well and I spent most of my time in the bar, getting smashed every weekend. Sometimes I drank so much I'd get home without knowing how I had gotten there. It got to the point where I'd drink a six-pack of beer for breakfast.

I smoked an occasional joint and took a pill every so often, slowly drifting back to heroin and the drug scene. My cousin was still in jail and I was waiting for him to get out, to see what his attitude would be like. I started going with several girls when I got out of the hospital but very few persons wanted to really bother with me. They knew I was a head.

One night when I was drinking in the bowling alley, four or five girls came in. They knew a couple of the guys I was with, although I had never seen any of them before. One girl struck me as being real good-looking. She had long black hair and was wearing sunglasses. I thought it was strange because the place we hung out in was as dark as Hernando's Hideaway on Saturday night, and I thought to myself, *What's with the shades?* I wondered if she was a head or not, but went over and introduced myself.

She told me her name was Margo. I asked if she wanted a drink, but she said no. We made small talk but since I had an appointment that night I had to leave. I told her I wanted to see her again.

About two weeks later a friend of mine came over and said, "All the guys who hang out in the bowling alley are going to Palisades Amusement Park. Would you like to go?" I told him I didn't go for that sort of thing. He said, "Margo, the girl you met at the bowling alley, might go with you if you'd call her up."

I was interested in seeing her again so I called her and she consented to go. We didn't go on any rides, just walked and talked, and because of that night, Margo and I became very good friends. Through her I got to know her grandmother, Mrs. Hannah Bowser and her mother, Mrs. Margaret Burkett. When I was dating Margo I broke over to narcotics quite a few times but nobody knew it.

Jackie came home from jail and I introduced him to Margo and her family. He was quite impressed with her mother and grandmother, because he had never met people like them before. He thought they were wonderful, sincere individuals. He still had a bit of larceny in his heart, though, and asked me if I was beating them for any money.

I laughed and said, "No, I'm not taking a thing from them." Most of the people we associated with were taken for something, their money or their pad, but I leveled with Margo's family. I saw in them a kind of peace, and they had real concern for me. They accepted me as a human being and showed me love.

Jackie broke over to narcotics a couple of times the first week he was home. We had asked him if he wanted to work on construction and he said yes, so Matty, my stepfather, got Jackie a job with us. We started to help each other and I saw Jackie desired to really get away from narcotics. On lunch breaks we'd stick close together. We had a good crew building the Lincoln Center for the Performing Arts. At noon Jackie and I would go to the hot dog stand for a few hot dogs and soda and watch the scenery.

Jackie told me he'd really like to stop using drugs. He said he had never expressed this to anyone before but a lot of things were bothering him. We both worked hard that first week together and Friday night I got paid, but Jackie had to wait till the next Friday for his paycheck. I asked him what he was going to do that night. It was a beautiful day in August. He answered, "Nothing."

I asked him, "Would you like to double-date with Margo and me?" He said he'd think about it.

After work we went over to his house. Our families had accepted us again because we both were working and, so far as they knew, were off drugs and really trying to make a go of it. Jackie and his father talked and joked around with each other. It seemed to be a perfect day, as though everything, at last, was going to work out for us. We were all out in Jackie's backyard drinking beer when the phone rang. Rose Marie answered it. She called Jackie, saying it was for him. I asked her who it was. She said, "It was a guy by the name of Mick."

I said, "You should never have given Jackie the phone, because Mick's a junkie." When Jackie came outside I asked him what Mick wanted. He said Mick called up to wish him luck since he knew Jackie was trying to go straight and was working.

Later, Jackie said he was going to get a haircut. I told him, "Listen, man, if you want to come with me tonight, by all means you're still welcome." He said he'd give me a call. We made arrangements with our uncles to go fishing the next day. Jackie was to call me at 4:30 Saturday morning. I left Jackie's house as he went off to get his haircut.

That evening, since I hadn't heard whether Jackie wanted to go with us or not, I went on to get Margo.

We had planned to see a movie. However, I said, "I'd rather not go to the movie tonight. If you don't mind, I'd like to look for Jackie." I had a strong feeling something was going to happen. She said she didn't mind, so we drove around looking for Jackie. In Corona, where all the hopheads hung out, the guys told me I had just missed him. I asked them who he was with and they said some blond-haired kid. I knew he was with Mick, the junkie. I told Margo, "I know something is going to happen to Jackie."

We drove to Forest Hills where there was another junkie hangout. Again, I learned we had missed Jackie by only a few minutes. That whole evening I combed New York City, just missing him by a few minutes at each place I went, so about midnight I took Margo home. I went home to bed, tossing restlessly before I fell into fitful sleep.

At 4:30 the next morning, the jangle of the telephone jerked me awake. The caller was my cousin Ella, Jackie's sister, crying hysterically, "Jackie is dead! Jackie is dead!" I tried to tell her how to bring him out of an OD (overdose) by giving him a shot of salt water and putting him in a cold shower. But she sobbed, "It's too late! The coroner has already taken him away!"

I was stunned beyond words. I was too stunned even to cry out. My mother heard me talking to Ella on the phone and she started crying bitterly, but we didn't know what to say to each other. We decided the best thing would be to dress and go to my aunt's house because we knew they would need help. We hurried to the house where my uncle was threatening revenge, talking wildly out of his head because he had just lost his only son. My sister was crying hysterically, and it was a grief-stricken situation. I felt alone!

It was the first time in my life I had ever felt really alone. Many times when I was high in the city with nine million people around me, I felt lonely. But I knew I had a friend, I knew I had someone: Jackie. But now I had only emptiness.

I slipped away from the commotion and went to Jackie's room, threw myself across his bed, and cried, and cried, and cried! A crucifix hung on his wall and I started to pray to the crucifix and to kiss it, trying to repent for all Jackie had done. I thought I should go to the church and light a few candles. I hurried to the church. I don't know why, but probably Jackie's death made me feel closer to God. I started praying at the church, not for myself, but for Jackie and for his soul, not knowing where he was.

Later we found out what had happened. Mick's wife found both Mick and Jackie dead in her apartment. Expecting their first child within two months, she went into severe shock. The police were called. Meanwhile, Jackie's mother decided to go to Mick's apartment to see if Jackie was there. There she was met by two officers. The expressions on their faces told her something was wrong.

Shoving the brawny men aside, she pushed her way into the bathroom where Jackie lay on the floor—dead. Mick's body had been found on the living room floor. Dark stains on the carpet spoke of massive hemorrhaging which preceded death.

I went off by myself and thought about the dream I'd had of Jackie dying. I suddenly realized I'd had that dream exactly one year ago to the day! Now, according to the dream, in six months I would die! Chills ran up and down my spine and I thought, *If I'm going to die in six months, I'd better prepare myself for death.* That night, my whole family went over to the funeral parlor. I was even scared to look at the nameplate over the viewing room door in the funeral parlor. I saw Jackie's name and a huge lump stuck in my throat.

I felt very nervous as I walked into the room where Jackie was laid out. I looked at him, still handsome, but dead, exactly the way I had seen him in my dream with his green suit, black shoes, white shirt, the whole thing. I broke up, my emotions running away with me. I knew I had to get myself together so, after the wake, I went to a bar and started drinking. I drank and drank but couldn't get drunk. As a matter of fact, the liquor didn't even taste good. I went home, got out my rosary beads, and prayed.

The body was not permitted to be taken into the Catholic church. We asked why, since it was an accidental death, and were told it was because of the way he had died. The priest agreed to allow a mass to be said for him in the church, for a certain amount of money. My aunt paid to have the mass said. The priest was very nice, and helpful to my aunt in her grief. But, because they wouldn't allow my cousin's remains in the church, I swore I'd never set foot inside a Catholic church again, yet I prayed faithfully.

After Jackie was buried, I tried to do the right thing. I had many long talks with Margo's mother. And I talked to her grandmother quite often about death. Grandma Bowser, a consistent Christian, often told me of Christ and how wonderful his life was. Life for me, I knew, had to begin soon to make sense. I felt I was running out of time; like an hourglass with only a few grains of sand to trickle out.

At this period in my life, I was doing a lot of drinking. I enticed Margo to start drinking and she was actually becoming a booze head. I learned she was only sixteen years old when I started going with her. She had lied to me at first, saying she was eighteen, so we began going to nightclubs. Margo and I became rather serious so I told her the whole story of my life, my drug problem and everything. I concluded with, "If you don't want to see me again I wouldn't blame you." She said she thought I had better tell her mother about my background. I did.

54   Her mother said that if I was off drugs, it was okay for Margo and me to date. We dated and had very good times together. Her grandmother Bowser often talked to me about Jesus Christ. When she first started about this Jesus I didn't want to listen—after what happened to Jackie and what the chaplain had told me in jail. I felt it wasn't for me, and even though I had sworn off the Catholic church, I was still a member of it, and Margo's family was Protestant. Still grandma kept telling me about Jesus.

When I would go pick Margo up for a date, she'd be late, giving grandma a chance to talk with me about Jesus Christ. Then I started asking questions about Jesus. I caught myself hoping Margo wouldn't be ready for our date, just so I could hear more about Jesus. At this time I was still using drugs and drinking a lot, but neither Margo nor her grandma knew anything about the drugs. I cheated on Margo, going out with different girls. Margo thought she was going to be able to change me. At the beginning, even I thought she might be able to do just that. But that was more than I should have expected.

One night, after coming back from a booze session we had with our friends, I became furious with Margo because I thought she was making eyes at one of my friends. Numbed by liquor, I smacked her across the mouth. I finally came to my senses and apologized to her and asked her if she'd forgive me. She said she would never take another drink of liquor as long as she lived and that I had better stop too. I didn't stop but she did, and from then on she wanted nothing to do with liquor.

Summer was soon over and the fall months were at hand. I was still working on construction and earning a lot of money. That whole winter I drank a lot, took pills, and smoked marijuana. When I dropped Margo off after our dates, I'd go with a friend to the city to a discotheque place and have a blast. Sometimes I'd stay out all night. Of course, Margo didn't know anything about it and I didn't plan on her finding out.

Three days before New Year's Eve in 1963 some friends bought some Scotch and came to my house. We all went to the basement and started drinking. I drank a whole bottle of Scotch, becoming so drunk and sick that I was sick right up to New Year's Eve, which became the soberest New Year's Eve I'd had in years! I didn't touch a drink, didn't even want to look at any. I thought that was the end of my drinking career because I had gotten too sick to drink anymore. My liver was bothering me because while using heroin I had gotten hepatitis, probably from a dirty needle. Drug users are subject not only to hepatitis but, even worse, syphilis.

When I was using drugs I knew girls who had babies born as infa-addicts. About ten minutes after the baby was born, he'd go into a convulsion, craving narcotics. The medical experts at one time didn't know what was wrong with these babies but have recently learned they crave narcotics because of their parents' habits. These babies were born infa-addicts.

One girl, an LSD user, and her common-law husband, also a user, had a baby. The child was born an "it." The child had a normal head but just a lump of flesh for a body—no arms, no legs, nothing to identify it as male or female.

Although I knew I was living dangerously, I continued on drugs and drinking. I was hooked, but good.

4

A New Kind of High

One evening late in January my aunt called to ask if I would take her to see her son, who was in a boys' reformatory. I had taken her there previously. However, I had quickly tired of sitting in the reception room waiting for her visit to end. So this time I asked two friends along to keep me company. One of the boys, Bucky, took along a shotgun and we had target practice while my aunt visited her son.

We had great fun in the woods, shooting at various targets or anything that moved. I had a camera and we goofed around taking pictures. It was quite a nice day, but cold, and there was snow on the ground. We were up in the Catskill Mountains and glad to be away from the snarling rush of New York City. All too soon, the time came for us to meet my aunt at the reformatory and return home.

At home that night before dinner, two boys, Reuben, a Puerto Rican, Bucky, and I started drinking a gallon of Italian wine. We had drunk quite a bit of it when my mother came home from work and prepared dinner for us. After dinner, Bucky, Reuben, and I went to the local hangout, a dirty old bar. Most of the men who drank there had domestic problems, or lived by themselves and were very lonely. Before long other guys who hung out with us drifted into the bar and we started to drink quite heavily. A singing group in our crowd began to sing rock-and-roll songs and we all had a blast just singing and dancing. A few girls were singing and drinking right along with us.

About 11:30 I decided to go home. After midnight Bucky and another fellow came to my house to get the shotgun we had used that day. They asked me if I wanted to go to the Bronx with them to return the shotgun to Bucky's uncle. I hurried into my clothes. We started driving toward the Bronx, feeling pretty good from the drinks we had had that day.

As we entered the Whitestone Bridge from a side street, a car backed out in front of us from a driveway. Instead of stopping to give the man the right-of-way, we blew the horn and yelled at him. The driver, who had a woman with him, jumped out of the other car, swearing loudly. He was a huge Negro man. I weighed about two hundred and stood just under six feet, yet he towered over me. He whipped out a knife and growled, "If any of you wants to challenge me, get out of the car and do it!" Seeing the knife, I froze.

As the man stalked away from our car there was silence. Suddenly something came over me and I growled, "Get him! Get him!" Since we had the shotgun in the car, I thought maybe I could bluff this guy. I wanted to make him back down because my ego was hurt. He gunned his car out ahead of us, so I yelled to Bucky, "Get him!" All Bucky needed was encouragement, so we shot out after the speeding car.

Racing along the Whitestone Expressway, we cut the man off and stopped. I grabbed the shotgun and held it up to his face. For a moment he hesitated. Out of the corner of my eye I saw cars pull off the side of the highway and stop. Then the man came after me, apparently realizing the gun was not loaded. If that gun had been loaded, I would have blown off his head, without the slightest hesitation.

That huge, strong man jerked that shotgun away from me as though it were a toy. He pulled out his knife and slashed down, aiming at my face. I threw up my arm in defense. The knife ripped through my overcoat, sweater, shirtsleeve, and gouged a long slash on my arm.

After he stabbed me, he went after Bucky, stabbing under the arm, ripping the underarm severely. I heard a tormented scream, "Vince! He got me!"

When I heard that I went berserk. Cursing the Negro, I grabbed the shotgun. The man was on top of Bucky, ready to stab him again. Raising the gun above my head, I came down as hard as I could. After I hit him, the man just looked at me. I hit him over the head again, splintering the stock of the gun into several pieces. The man fell over on his back. His eyes rolled back. I thought he was dead.

He lay on his back, arms stretched out and legs crossed. To my fuzzy mind, it looked like Christ on the cross. Something very peculiar came over me. I took the man's knife, wanting to stick it through his hands. Why I wanted to do it, I'll never know. However, when my friends saw what I wanted to do, they thought I was crazy. Bucky, who was stabbed severely, helped Tommy pull me off the man, who we thought was dead. Climbing into our car, we noticed there were about forty cars lining the roadside, their drivers watching our every move. Yet nobody made an attempt to stop us.

59

We took off and went to a friend's house to get first aid. There I looked at Bucky's wound and it made me sick. When he lifted his arm, I could see inside the pit of his arm and even his rib cage. We all knew it was a very serious wound.

We told Bucky to go to the hospital alone. We couldn't go with him because if a doctor were to see my cut and Bucky's stab wound, he would know we had been in a rumble and the police would be notified. We didn't want that. Bucky took me home, then drove to a hospital.

I shaved around the cut on my arm, washed it with peroxide, poured Mercurochrome on it, and taped a

Band-Aid on it. My cut wasn't too deep but it was still pretty bad. I started to smoke, worried about what I had done to that man, thinking he must have died. Then I started talking to God. I didn't know how to pray, but I told him if he would spare this man's life, I would surrender my all to him. The little religious training I'd had gave me guilt feelings about what I'd done. I had been going to church in Yonkers, and had met some wonderful people. Now I was afraid that if they ever found out what I had done tonight, they would not want me there. They knew I wasn't a Christian, but because of my phony front, this was something they wouldn't think I would stoop to do.

That night I prayed sincerely for that man to live. While I prayed and smoked a cigarette my sister Rose Marie came home. I told her what had happened. She thought I should get out of the country until this thing blew over. I decided that if the man was dead, I was going to give myself up to the police. And if he lived, I was going to stop all my troublemaking. So, after a long talk with my sister, I finally went to sleep.

I woke up early the next morning and called Bucky to see what had happened at the hospital. He said he had quite an experience. He told them he had been drinking and had fallen, cutting his armpit on a broken beer bottle. They apparently believed his story. However, while Bucky was in the emergency room, the Negro man I had hit was lying on the opposite side of the curtain, being taken care of. Asking about the man, Bucky was told he had a concussion. I thanked God it was no more than that. Bucky said that when he saw the man lying there, he became petrified.

That day I went back to the bar, where all the guys congratulated me on my accomplishment. They thought I was a big hero. That was not my feeling, though. I told Bucky I was quitting the gang, giving it up completely. So I broke away from the guys that night and stayed by myself. I sat in the house and did nothing.

The weather was so bad there was little construction work. I became bored and eventually drifted back to the gang. During this period I was going to church in Yonkers. I didn't tell Mrs. Bowser what had happened because I was ashamed. I didn't want to lower her opinion of me. On Sunday mornings I would pick up Mrs. Bowser, her daughter, and granddaughters and we would go to church. After service one Sunday a young man named Ernie came over to me. Ernie was the youth leader and knew me just slightly, but he asked me if I would go to a youth rally and retreat sponsored by the church.

I told him, "Thanks for the offer, but that isn't my bag. Religion on Sunday is okay, but on Friday, Saturday, Sunday, and Monday! That would be too much for me. Besides I would feel out of place, like a sixth finger on a hand." I thanked him again for the offer but told him definitely no.

Something about the church was really starting to bug me. These people seemed to enjoy life—without liquor, narcotics, or immorality. I saw something in their lives I craved, but did not know how to go about getting it. I thought you worked your way into being a self-righteous person by doing good things and that this was how they obtained what they had.

Monday came, and still no work, so I went out with the boys again. We got some marijuana and smoked it, and used some goofballs. This was the process of the whole week. One night we were sitting in my car drinking cheap wine, singing, goofing around. We talked about God and I bragged about all the knowledge I had received from attending church and talking with Mrs. Bowser. Little did I know that even then the Holy Spirit was working on me.

While we were drinking and talking about the church and religious matters, a fellow we called Spanish John came bombing up to the car, saying, "Who needs nylons for his girl friend?" I looked at him and called him a heathen. He stared at me, a blank expression on his face, and said, "Man, what are you calling me a heathen for?"

I asked him, "Did you steal those nylons?" He replied that he had boosted them from the corner drugstore. I said, "God is going to punish you for that."

I was only joking with him but he said, "What do you mean, God is going to punish me?"

I said, "Don't you know the Bible says 'Thou shall not steal'? You ought to go take them back. You're afraid to take them back, aren't you?"

"Do you believe in God?" he asked.

Serious, I replied, "Yes, I do believe in God."

"If you believe in God so much, why don't you come back to the drugstore with me?" So I agreed. Half drunk, I walked back to the drugstore with John.

We went to the manager of the store and John said, "Mister, I robbed these nylons from your store and I believe in God so I want to give them back." He made the sign of the cross. I almost cracked up when he did this. The manager looked at him, astonishment written on his face.

He mumbled, "Thanks for bringing them back" and then he just stared, at a loss for words. John and I walked out, climbed into the car, and off we went.

That night Ernie, the youth leader, called again and asked if I would go to Rochester, N.H., with the church youth group. I told him I still didn't want to go so he hung up. I called Margo and told her what Ernie said. She said she wanted to go, so we both decided we'd go if Ernie called again. He did call—three times in one night—and I said we would go. We were to leave Friday afternoon, February 23.

That afternoon finally came and as I was sitting in my living room, smoking, I felt very strange inside. I thought, *Something is going to happen to me.*

I asked Rose Marie to take Margo and me to the Bronx to meet Ernie. As we drove along the Major Deegan Expressway I puffed on a cigarette and decided that since I respected the church people, I would not smoke in front of them.

We met Ernie on Jerome Avenue in the Bronx and were soon off in his car to Rochester, N.H. Now I was away from drugs, booze, and all that goes with it. On the drive to Rochester I noticed the sky, thinking how red it was. I thought about all the friends I'd had— guys I knew who were not living anymore because of narcotics. I thought how fortunate I was to be going away, getting out of the city. I realized there were people in the world who cared for me as an individual. And with these pleasant thoughts I dozed off to sleep.

About five hours later we arrived in Rochester, N.H., stopping at a big white house. There I met Rev. and Mrs. Bill Clock. My first impression of Mrs. Clock was that she was an old hag who didn't know what she was talking about. I hated Mrs. Clock the first time I saw her. She had a very domineering manner, I thought. Drifting off in the background, I stayed alone.

The next day we had a discussion on ethics. We talked about how girls should dress and how boys and girls should conduct themselves. Mrs. Clock said she didn't think girls should wear dresses above their knees or low-cut dresses. I asked her who she thought she was to tell the girls how to dress and act. My opinion was about as popular as a nest of rattlesnakes.

After the discussion session, they had recreation. It was the first time I had ever been tobogganing and we all had a real good time. Several of us went down on a toboggan together. We wiped out people all over the ice and had a real blast. I watched these other kids and they too were really enjoying themselves. This was the first time in a long while I could honestly say I had a good time without drinking, smoking, fighting, or girl-chasing. I thought there must be something more to life than drugs and emptiness.

That night after recreation a hayride was on the agenda. The kids were goofing off and I was really digging them. I really watched to see if they were sincere in this thing of Christianity. On this hayride the group sang songs—they called them choruses. It was a beautiful night with stars studding the velvety sky. The kids sang "Give me oil in my lamp, keep me burning, burning, burning." I started to join in with them, feeling very stupid, mind you. I thought, *Here*

I am tonight singing Give me oil in my lamp, keep me burning, burning, burning, and last night I was standing on the corner singing Give me booze and drugs, keep me going, going, going. I really enjoyed myself, though I tried not to.

Two voices seemed to speak to me on that hayride. One seemed to say, "Vince, get off this wagon, go to a bus depot, and go back to N.Y.C. where you belong. You don't have any right being here with these people." But another voice seemed to whisper, "I will watch over you. I love you." For a minute I thought I was cracking up. Then the hayride was over and we all went back to the cars.

Ernie discovered he had locked the keys in his car with the motor running. I said under my breath, "You idiot. You knew what you were doing." For the moment all the good accomplished on the hayride was blotted out by this incident with the car keys. It wasn't Ernie's fault—it could have happened to anyone. But I was mad. Before long we got another key from Ernie's wife and drove back to the church.

When we got there the young people were in the sanctuary singing choruses. I didn't want anything to do with it so I went downstairs and sat around by the fireplace, drinking hot chocolate with some of the other misfits who were with us. Who should come walking down the steps to the basement? Mrs. Clock, big mouth herself! She said, "You young people should go upstairs and sing with the others. The singing is glorious." I walked out of the church in a rage. I was getting back to being my old self.

After the worship service that night we were assigned to various homes to spend the night. I went to an old, but well-kept farmhouse where an elderly lady lived with her son. She treated us like royalty, yet I searched her drawers and closets to see what I could take. There was nothing of much value. I asked if I could take a bath. The woman said yes and got out towels for me.

I shared the room with Phil Nassar, but since I was tired, I cut our conversation short. As I dropped my head on the pillow I said to myself, "Mrs. Clock, let me alone," and went to sleep. The next morning I woke up, feeling rather strange, unexplainable but with great anticipation.

I went downstairs to a breakfast fit for a king: eggs, bacon, toast, coffee, milk, homemade preserves—the works. I thought to myself, *Man, this is too much. This lady doesn't even know me, yet she made me a breakfast like this!*

Phil and I chowed down and went on to church where Bill Clock was holding Sunday school classes. This was the first time I had ever been in a Sunday school class. I had attended church but never Sunday school. Once when I was small I had gone to a Protestant church by mistake and had been put in a Sunday school class. This was altogether different.

They talked about Jesus, belief, the power God has, why he sent his Son to earth. This was new to me. As a kid I went to Catechism, but we didn't learn the importance of a personal encounter with Christ. Now as I heard it, it sounded strange and foreign to me. I enjoyed Sunday school, especially after I got up enough courage to ask a couple of questions. After Sunday school, Pastor Clock prepared for the morning worship. I sat in that old church building and thought,

How different! There was a reverence about the entire service and the music and singing were altogether different. The sermon was about trusting and accepting God and his promises. Rev. Clock seemed to be preaching straight at me. He told of some experiences he had on the mission field in Pakistan.

One story was about a woman whose daughter was sick. The missionary said to this woman, "Why don't you pray to Jesus and give up your idols? God will meet your need. Place your trust in him." This woman gave up her idols and prayed to Jesus. But when God answered her prayers, she went back to her idols.

I thought, *That sounds like me. I pray to God and when he answers my prayers, I go back to my idols—drugs, booze, broads.* This thought hit me like a pile-driver. I thought for a long while on that, hearing little of the rest of the sermon. Before I knew it the sermon was over. We sang a song that said, "Only trust him, Only trust him, . . . He will save you now." That word *trust* was the key word of the whole sermon. Trust. During my life I had trusted so many people—friends, relatives, but it seemed so many had let me down. But there was one I had never trusted and that was the Son of God, Jesus Christ. I wondered, *Should I trust him?*

As I was pondering what to do a voice seemed to say, "Vince, get out of this church. If you listen to this preacher, you'll never be accepted by the gang. You'll never be able to go back to drugs, to the orgies you've had. Your whole life will be revolutionized. Go ahead. Get out of here, you don't belong here!"

I started to weep for some unknown reason, but another still, quiet voice seemed to say, "I love you, and I want you. Come!" And Rev. Clock said, "Come. Accept Jesus Christ as your Lord and Savior."

I felt as if the floor of the church had tilted and was pushing me into the aisle. Before I knew it I found myself standing in the aisle of the church. I stumbled my way to the altar. I didn't know why, but I was crying. I knelt to pray. I didn't know how to pray or what to pray for. I thought I'd never be able to make it because I had too much against me. But then the love of God came into my heart full-strength and I knew Jesus Christ had freed me.

While I was at the altar I sensed that God was telling me to get more education. I thought of how I had to get back to work, so when the minister said, "Son, is there a need in your life?" I looked up, with tears streaming, and said, "Yeah, I need a job." He looked at me as though I were some kind of weirdo.

He prayed with me, though, and I started to cry again. After the prayer, I got up and started to shake hands with people I'd never met before. I looked at Mrs. Clock and I didn't feel at all the same way I had felt about her before. Remembering that dream I had had about my cousin Jackie and me dying, I figured the time. It was six months to the day since my cousin's death. I really had died—to self—and was born again into the kingdom of God.

We were scheduled to leave Rochester at noon and I couldn't wait to get home and tell people what had happened to me. Driving back to N.Y.C. we listened to Dr. Norman Vincent Peale and Billy Graham on the radio. I started to cry again, but nothing mattered anymore except my doing God's will. I wondered why I had never really heard these messages before.

I felt like a new person; God really had worked in my life. I was like a new creation. I had read in the Bible the statement, "If anyone is in Christ, he is a new creation; the old has passed away, behold, the new has come" (2 Cor. 5:17). This was exactly what I was experiencing. All my old desires were gone and new ideas and ambitions were starting to come into my life.

I could hardly wait to tell my mother I had become a Christian and to see what her reaction would be. When we reached my house I walked in the door and saw mom sitting on the couch. I swallowed and said, "Guess what happened to me!"

She gave me a puzzled look and said, "I don't know. What?" I told her I had given my heart to the Lord, I had been saved. She simply said, "So what?"

She didn't know the term *saved* or what it meant, so I said, "Mom, that means I'm not going to smoke, drink booze, or use drugs anymore. I belong to God now and God is going to watch over me." She found this difficult to believe or accept. I looked at my Christian friends and said, "I'll never make it."

One of them said to me, "Don't place your faith in man, but keep your eyes and faith on the Son of God." Fortunately, I held to that advice.

I couldn't wait to get over to see Mrs. Bowser. I went to her home that night. Wisely, she knew when I walked in that something had happened. I looked at her and said, "Grandma, guess what?"

Her eyes wide with anticipation, she said, "What?"

"I gave my heart to the Lord. I'm a Christian!"

She clapped her hands and said, "Praise the Lord! This is an answer to prayer!" I believed that, because a lot of fine Christian people had been praying for me. After receiving hearty congratulations, I had prayer with Mrs. Bowser and her family, then left.

That night I could hardly sleep, so great was the joy that swelled my heart. But I knew I had a mission to accomplish for God. I had a mother, sister, father, and stepfather who needed to know Christ. My radical conversion was not easy for them to understand. Once, Rose Marie said to a friend, "My brother is not a Roman Catholic nor is he a Protestant. He is a Christian." And this is what I hoped to reveal to my parents through the power of the Holy Spirit.

However, I needed to work, to keep my mind occupied, because I had a long road ahead of me. I knew temptation would be upon me and I could very easily slip and fall back to where I had left off in my old life. So I began to pray that God would send me work. While I was off work, I read the Gospel of John several times. This gave me strength and courage.

5

A Long Way to Grow

In a very few days I received a telephone call from a foreman asking me to come to work. I went back to work on construction, and I think that because of my Christian experience I became a better worker. Sometimes accidents occurred on a job. A finger might be smashed or a toe stubbed on a piece of steel, and the injured man would blurt out swear words. Yet, when this happened to me, I didn't curse anymore or become angry. I just accepted it as an accident, knowing such things do happen. Little did I know, though, that my fellow workers were watching me.

They had known me when I used to drink, use the needle, and take other barbiturates and stimulants. Now they saw that I didn't drink or smoke. One day a foreman yelled down at me, "Hey you, Vince. Don't you ever swear?"

I looked up at him and said, "There's no need to swear." And I simply told him I had the love of God in my heart. He didn't understand. Of course, he mocked this love, yet he respected me in his own way. He was an alcoholic, and I told him many times that in order for him to get off booze it would take the power of God, nothing less. However, I still had to go back to the gang and tell them.

One night I went into the bar where the gang were all drinking and talking. When I ordered a Coke they laughed at me, asking if I was on the wagon. I told them plainly that I had given my heart to the Lord and had become a Christian. I advised them to do the same thing. Many of them were dumbfounded. Some snickered and laughed, saying I had "got religion." They said, "Oh, you'll be back to your old ways in a couple of months. This won't last."

I said, "No, this is the real thing." I told them how wonderful it was to have a personal relationship with Jesus Christ, the Son of God. The bartender listened attentively and, after I finished talking with the boys, he came over to me, shook my hand and said, "Congratulations, Vince. I hope you keep it up." With that I left the guys and went home.

From my initial experience on, I was able to overcome temptation through a personal relationship with God. I knew I would have to receive help through reading the Bible, through developing a deep attitude of prayer, and complete commitment to God.

My church had no pastor so I accepted much of the responsibility there. Right away, with help from an experienced teacher, I began to teach a Sunday school class. This helped me to grow in a hurry. I felt inferior to some of the children in my class because they had attended church since infancy. I was twenty-four years old and just learning to read the Bible. Only through the power and guidance of God was I able to sit down, study, discipline my life. This discipline was soon to become indispensable for me.

Because of my involvement in Christian work, I was no longer bored or disgusted with life. Something gave me meaning, purpose, direction, goal, all the things I had longed for in my old life but never had been able to achieve. While my greatest ambition had been to become a racketeer, now something new and alive was in me. I tried to share it with my associates on the construction job and during my social times.

Of course, many rejected what I had to say. Feelings ran high among my own relatives. They were afraid I had changed my religion. I told them I hadn't changed my faith at all, I had just increased it. One uncle said, "Before I would change my religion I would rather go to hell." I realized that was a real possibility. However, this same uncle now insists upon my praying before he will eat a meal at which I am present.

My becoming a Christian gave me more incentive to work. Before I became a Christian, I disliked manual labor, was lazy, and had no motivation. After my conversion I took on more responsibilities. I became less rebellious and more secure. Anyway, construction pay was good; I was making more than one hundred and fifty dollars a week and for some reason I felt that I should save as much as I possibly could. Still I had no idea what God wanted me to do as a lifework.

I found many opportunities to share with others what God had done for me. On one construction job, during coffee break, a number of the fellows who heard that I had "got religion" came over to me and wanted to know about it. I told them about conversion, about my personal trust and faith in Jesus Christ and my accepting him as Lord and Savior. Some of them were very interested and, of course, there were some who sneered. But many questions were asked about conversion, the reality of God, how I knew there was a God. I felt there was no need for me to defend God. I simply shared my experience and beliefs.

These men were asking questions because they were inquisitive and really wanted to know. I felt they were honestly seeking to know God or wanting God to reveal himself to them. I knew he would in his own time and it wasn't up to me; my obligation was to tell them what had happened to my life. I really liked construction work and my fellow workers. They were a good bunch of guys. Some of them had had bad breaks right from childhood up, even as I had. I still think about them and pray for them, trusting that God in his infinite mercy will someday find an open door into their hearts.

One bad feature about construction work is that it is seasonal. During January and February following my conversion, work slackened quite a bit and many of the men were laid off. During that time of idleness I read as much literature as I could get. I studied a great deal about what God had to say in his Word. A friend of mine gave me a book entitled *The Cross and the Switchblade*. The book revealed ways God guides and directs people who are open to him. I decided to go to Teen Challenge and investigate its ministry. Being an ex-addict, I found appeal in this type of ministry and I thought perhaps I might be of some help in the work there. I called Teen Challenge and talked to Mr. Don Wilkerson, Dave's brother. When I asked if I could visit the rehabilitation center, he invited me to come. There I met a lot of fellows who knew associates of mine. The staff at Teen Challenge made me feel right at home.

I fitted in with fellows who, like myself, were uneducated, ex-drug addicts. They had been outcasts from society. Something new had taken over their lives and they were transformed by the wonderful gospel of Jesus Christ.

Taken on a tour of the center, I was amazed at the way these converted drug addicts stuck together and prayed for one another. It was remarkable and a great inspiration to see young guys on their knees, calling upon God for help, not ashamed to pray. Completely taken up with the idea of Teen Challenge, I asked if I could visit again. I went back several times. Then one day I told Don Wilkerson, "If you need me or my car, I would be glad to help out."

His reply was, "This is an answer to prayer. We have been looking for a single fellow for our staff. We definitely can use you. You are welcome to live with us at the center." That began my work there.

While there I had many opportunities to talk to addicts who were not yet converted but who in time became Spirit-filled Christians. I really loved these guys, and I tried to understand them and their needs. One fellow, Johnny De Jesus, told me I understood them more than other people did, because I was an ex-junkie myself and I knew what the score was.

I asked a number of the boys exactly why they had become drug users. Their replies were shocking. One boy said he really didn't have too much to live for. His mother was a prostitute and from childhood he had seen her bring men home and go to bed with them. Another said he was in bed, along with his sister, and his mother and her boyfriend were in the same bed. Situations like these plagued their minds and disturbed their emotions. They felt the drugs they used pushed these things far back in their minds. Heroin became a crutch, an escape from reality.

Many of the young men I met told me their lack of education caused them to become drug addicts. They felt insecure, or felt the sting of racial prejudice. Drugs clouded their problems—at first.

One of the greatest experiences I witnessed at Teen Challenge was when a young man, Charlie, came strutting into the Center early one morning. I looked at this fellow, a real mean-looking guy, who said, "I want to see the director." I took him into the office of Don Wilkerson. We talked to this fellow, asking him how old he was when he began using drugs.

Charlie told us he was twelve years old when he started and now he was a heroin user, a mainliner. We asked him if he had any narcotics on him— standard procedure at Teen Challenge—or hypodermic needles, pot, or works. Clients have to turn in cigarettes, liquor, and any weapons.

When we asked him if he had any weapons on him, he stared at us for a moment, then lifted his pant leg, and pulled out a knife with a ten- or eleven-inch blade. Don and I looked at each other and grinned. I took Charlie upstairs and got him squared away. He would have a tough four days to face because he was going to kick his heroin habit cold. I knew what was going to happen to him, the pain he was going to undergo. But I knew that if he meant business and wanted to get off drugs, this was the only way to have a victory.

For four days Charlie lay in bed while he withdrew, with no medication at all. I witnessed several of these withdrawals without medication and learned that sometimes God is so merciful some of the kids have very little withdrawal pain. Charlie came downstairs after four days. I asked him how he felt and he said, "pretty weak." So I took him to get some food. In another week Charlie regained his strength and was able to function normally.

However, the mental craving was still there and he felt he needed a fix to be straightened out. Knowing this boy had been an addict for nine or ten years, I prayed that God would speak to Charlie's heart, and Charlie would let Christ help him. Other fellows at the center also prayed for him.

One night we went to Staten Island to a service in one of the churches there. All the fellows from the

Center went to the service. During the service I prayed earnestly that Charlie would open his heart to the Lord that night. At the end of the sermon an invitation was given and, while I was praying, Charlie got up and made his way to the altar. He fell to his knees and started praying. I went up and knelt beside him. He looked at me and said, "Vince, now I realize why we are put here on this earth."

I asked him, "Why, Charlie? Why do you think we're put on this earth?"

He replied, "To worship and serve the Lord Jesus Christ." Well, Charlie and I prayed the prayer of faith and he accepted Christ—or so I thought. The next morning Charlie came over to me and said, "You know, I feel like a real jerk. Last night that was nothing but sheer emotion. I didn't get saved at all. A lot of tension had built up in me through the years and I just let it all out last night."

I said, "Don't think that just because you had a lot of emotion God didn't work with you. You said something many Christian people do not realize, something about being put here on earth to serve the Lord."

He only looked at me and gave me the wave-off. That afternoon he called me aside and told me he could never become a Christian. When I asked him why, he said that when he was on the street, one of the ways he got money was to go into church vestibules and steal watches and rings. Since some churches didn't like for worshippers to wear jewelry, many people would take off watches, rings, and necklaces and hide them in their coat pockets till church was over. Charlie said, "In some of these churches the

77

pickings were real good, but now I feel God could never forgive me for stealing out of churches."

I told him of the Apostle Paul, how he hated and persecuted Christians, but yet God was merciful to him. I pressed the point by saying, "If God was merciful enough to forgive Paul, I'm sure he is merciful enough to forgive you, Charlie."

Charlie just looked at me but didn't say much. That night in chapel the singing was especially good. The Teen Challenge chaplain was to speak to the group. After the song service, Charlie whispered to me, "I'm not going through this again!" He strode out of the chapel and into the recreation room where he sat on the couch. After chapel was over, two boys walked into the recreation room where they found Charlie on his knees, crying bitterly.

The boys called me into the room. I asked Charlie what had happened. He said, "How stupid of me to deny that God touched me last night. Tonight I didn't sit in chapel yet the very same thing happened here in the quiet of this room. God touched me." Charlie then accepted Jesus Christ as his Lord and Savior. His face fairly shone with relief and joy.

Some of the boys at the Center were given privileges to visit their families. The conditions in which some of these fellows lived were deplorable. It almost seemed they were destined to become drug addicts. There was very little incentive to give the people courage. Most lived from one welfare check to the next. Conditions were worse than unsanitary.

I once accompanied a boy to his home in a rundown tenement house. My skin seemed to crawl as soon as

I entered the building, and after climbing several flights of dark and squeaky stairs, we came to this boy's apartment. His mother invited us in and offered us seats. Carefully avoiding a soft chair, I made my way to a wooden one in the corner.

The woman very kindly asked me if I would like some food. Staring at the swarm of cockroaches on the walls, I felt a lump come up in my throat. I couldn't help but refuse the food. I did, however, accept a cup of tea. While I sipped my tea, observing silently, the young boy visited with his family.

One night I dreamed a young man was soon to come to the Center, a look-alike of my cousin Jackie, the boy who died from an overdose of narcotics. Early the next morning, I washed and dressed, and went downstairs to the recreation room. Sitting there was a strange young man, yet not really strange since he was like the boy I had dreamed about. He looked a lot like Jackie. Immediately I took a liking to the boy. His name was Johnny.

Johnny told me he had heard about the work of Teen Challenge through an inmate at Rikers Island. When Johnny was discharged from Rikers Island that morning he came straight to the Teen Challenge Center looking for help, both spiritual and educational. Of course he wasn't a Christian yet, but that night during chapel service, Johnny went forward to pray. I was privileged to help lead him to Christ.

After chapel that night a group of the fellows got together for a prayer meeting. Just a group of guys from the inner city, knowing very little about theology or the proper way of praying, we formed a prayer circle, and began to thank and praise the Lord for the many blessings he had given us in the short while we were at the center. We had a marvelous time in the Lord. Although we prayed for about two hours, it seemed as if we prayed only ten minutes.

Many other addicts I knew and worked with came from elite parts of Westchester County and the residential sections of Queens, such as Forest Hills, Jamaica Estates, Malba, and other communities. Drugs, I learned, respected no person. But, then, neither is God a respecter of persons.

My call to the Christian ministry came while I was working on construction. One blistering hot day we were on a job in Jamaica, in Queens. I was putting in reinforcing steel. Joking, I said to one of the workers beside me, "We ought to find a new profession."

Looking up at me he said, "What?" then, laughing, "Yeah. You ought to become a preacher."

I laughed and said, "Stop joking around."

He said, "No, I'm not joking in the least. You have the physical qualifications, at least."

That rather struck me and then, that same morning, another young fellow said to me, "Vince, have you ever given any thought to becoming a minister?"

Well, I had, but not to any depth. At noon, instead of going with the other workers to the diner, I felt I should pray, seek God's guidance concerning the future of my life, whether he wanted me in the ministry or not. I knew any decision could lead to a great step and possibly a hard road. Never more sincere, I went off by myself. I found a bench overlooking a little gully and there sat to pray and seek God's guidance. I closed my eyes and bowed my head.

Not easily at first, the words came to my lips. "Dear Lord Jesus, if you want me to become a minister, please give some kind of sign. You know I am not well educated. I have a lot of shortcomings. Nevertheless, please make it known to me what you want me to be." With my head still bowed, I felt a warm breeze and a pressure like a hand on my shoulder. I turned around to see who was standing behind me. There was no one. I felt that experience was God's response to my asking him whether or not he wanted me to be a pastor.

That night I went to the midweek service at our church and, near the close, asked the minister if I could speak. He said to go right ahead, so I told the people about my experience on the job that day. No one showed great surprise; many people openly rejoiced. Apparently Pastor Price, a discerning man, sensed I would be called to the ministry, even before I knew it. His wife also confirmed it. Many people said, "We knew it all the while." A Mrs. Lowenstein said, "Vince, if you go to college, I'll pay for your books the first year." Doors began to open for my going to school.

I went to Mr. George Bowser one day and told him how uneducated I was, of the weak foundation I had for college. He said he felt if it was God's will that I go to college, he would give me the needed discipline, so I should not worry about it. When I shared my experience with some of my relatives, I received negative reactions. One uncle insisted I would never make it. But I told him that since God called me to the ministry, I was going to give it my very best. My sister, who was very concerned about my life, said, "Vince, do you really think you're going to do it? You know the handicap you have."

I said, "Rose Marie, if it is of God, I'll make it. If it isn't of God, then I will still gain by going to college to further my education." Like a young plant nourished by spring sun and rain, I was eager to grow—and I had a lot of growing to do.

6

Lightning Strikes Twice

Prior to my Teen Challenge days, I had gone steady with Margo, granddaughter of Mrs. Bowser. Margo became a Christian the same day I did, and after that we had many times of Bible reading and prayer together with Mrs. Bowser. However, when I went to Teen Challenge, my friendship with Margo became rather strained. I saw very little of her during those months and I felt she resented my living at Teen Challenge Center. Feeling that it was what the Lord wanted me to do at that particular time, I decided it was more important than anything else in my life—even Margo.

One evening Margo and I discussed the matter. I told her I felt I was where God wanted me. She didn't seem to understand. I also admitted that our future together was not as certain to me anymore.

We broke our engagement and I returned to Teen Challenge to work. Once, after discussing our future lives, we decided to go back together again.

Even though we tried to make a go at it the second time, things were never the same. Before Margo and I broke up the second time, we prayed much about it and came to the decision that it was not God's will for us to plan to be married.

Many people thought that, if we broke up, I would fall flat on my face, having no spiritual crutch. To their surprise—and mine—I became more zealous, more aggressive for Christ.

After leaving Teen Challenge, I went to live in Yonkers. There wasn't anyone to take care of the church property so the congregation asked me if I would live in the parsonage and lead the Wednesday evening services. Feeling this was the Lord's will, I accepted. I felt it was a time of spiritual growth.

Often, people of the church invited me to their homes for meals. But I think the times of greatest growth were when I was alone. I had much time to think and pray, to ask God to confirm my call to the ministry. I felt this was a task far beyond my capabilities. I really did not understand it all and did not know what God had in store for me. However, I stayed at the church in Yonkers for five months.

That winter I was active in the church in Yonkers. I lived in the church parsonage and worked as a counterman in the restaurant of a Christian man, Mr. George Nassar, Sr. He was a great inspiration to me and gave me a lot of good advice.

Summer was rapidly approaching and we advertised our area youth camp held at Conway, Massachusetts.

Ernie Rulli and I promoted the camp by asking kids in Yonkers to go to camp that summer. Before we knew it, July was upon us and we had quite a number of youth going to camp. There were about forty campers at our church camp, coming from several states.

The camp went quite smoothly and one night the director, Dr. Charles Clark, asked me if I would give the Friday vespers message. Since I had never preached before, I told him I was not experienced in this. But he seemed to think I was qualified to do it. I took the assignment seriously, giving every possible moment and thought to seek what God wanted me to tell those young people. I fasted, doing without food that whole day, and prayed.

That night, Friday, was Skit Night, with each cabin putting on a skit. The cooks served as judges to select the winner. After the skits, it was time for vespers. A young fellow named John Campetelle led the singing, and the kids really sang out. My hands felt clammy as I waited, even though I knew all the kids from Yonkers and had grown close to the others during the week. Finally called to speak, I rose knowing from the beginning God was with me.

Even though I knew nothing about sermon technique, I felt that God gave me guidance in delivering the message to the campers and to adult guests from various congregations. I told them what God had done in my life, comparing some of the disadvantages I had as a young person with the advantages many of them had. At the close of the service an invitation was given for young people to receive Christ.

About thirty came forward wanting to personally know Christ. My heart leaped as I saw those young people kneel to ask God to forgive them their sins. Those young people made some deep confessions that night. Many were troubled over wrongs they had done. One young man who had given us trouble that week came forward, weeping, crying out to the Lord, "Forgive me, forgive me for all the sins I have committed."

In the audience was a man who came over to me, threw his arms around me, and said, "I once made a statement about this camp that no one would ever become a Christian here." He marvelled that night to see all the young people who had responded. I, too, was thrilled to see what God had done. The next day that group went home and we counselors prepared for the senior high campers.

From thirteen to seventeen years of age, the senior campers were a bit more aggressive than the previous group and more sophisticated. I asked if they had any liquor, cigarettes, weapons, or anything of that nature. They said they were all clean, so I told them that, if I had to, I would frisk them. They insisted they did not have any stimulants or weapons on them.

The boys, normal, lively young fellows, wanted to raid the girls' cabin at night, an event which was against camp policy. Still one night, just to be safe, I asked them if they planned to pull a raid. Naturally all of them said no, so I went on to the counselors' meeting. During the meeting we heard people running around and girls screaming, so I went back to the cabin and counted heads. Everyone was there.

I thought for a minute and decided the boys should have some exercises that night—do some calisthenics to get the tension out of them. Walking over to one boy, I yanked the covers off him. He lay there fully clothed. I said to all those who had their clothes on, "Give me all your clothes, underwear included." I gathered up the clothes, took them to the dining hall, and that night there was no raid on the girls' cabin. Aside from this incident I really enjoyed having fun with the group of youths. Not too far from being a teen-ager myself, I really had a blast with those kids.

However, as the week progressed, Ken Crouch, assistant camp director, approached me to ask if I would again speak to the young people. I thought, *No, not these teen-agers,* because I wasn't too sure of myself. It was one thing to speak to eight- to twelve-year-olds, but this would be too difficult for me. Ken told me that if I was called to be a minister, I would have to be able to talk to young people. He said God would confirm his call to me by my speaking.

The day I was to preach, I again fasted, read the Bible, and prayed that whole day, trying to sense an outline to follow for my message to these young people. I knew I would have to get down to the nitty-gritty of life in order to affect these youths for God. That evening, John Campetelle led the singing. And what singing it was! We sang, "It's me, it's me, O Lord," and the kids really went for it because we speeded it up a bit, making it more to their liking.

Taking my text from John 3:3, I spoke about Nicodemus, about his need to be born again, and once again I felt confident. I knew God was speaking to many in that group. Knowing the disturbed home environment many of them came from, I really desired to see those young people accept help from Jesus

Christ. The Spirit was very evident that night. I noticed that even while I was preaching, a lot of young people were misty-eyed. I did not mean to play on their emotions, but I felt my words were from the Holy Spirit.

In my message, I told them about the environment I had grown up in, some of the difficulties I had faced, the hard times in school, my not being a good student. I told them about my life with drugs and how God miraculously delivered me. I closed with this statement, "I needed God in my life. And what you need is this very same Jesus."

The closing song was sung and an invitation given. I was never more earnest in prayer in my whole life than I was then. I saw one young man break for the altar, then another, and before long there were over thirty young people again at the altar. A young Christian named Vicky said, "I don't believe it. Lightning struck twice in the same place."

Many teen-agers made open confessions of how wrong they were in the life they had been living. One thirteen-year-old girl admitted going with boys down to the basement of her apartment building where they, in her words, "carried on," smoking and drinking. Several Catholic kids received Christ along with a lot of other young people. Out of that number at both camps, about fourteen young people from the church in Yonkers gave their hearts to Jesus Christ. Whether they all are now living for Christ, I can't say, but that night they came to grips with him.

While at camp at Roaring Brook, I met a young man called Richie, a most difficult young person to work with. He came from a home where Christ was not known, yet when I talked to this boy, he seemed to be calling out for help. I knew that the help he needed was the arm of love, the love Jesus Christ offers to a person who honestly seeks him.

I talked to Richard that night before evening vespers, asking him if he would accept Christ into his heart. He shook his head, saying, "No, I'm not ready."

I asked him if he loved God. He shrugged his shoulders. As I walked out of the cabin, I turned and said to him, "Richard, whether you love God or not, he loves you. Christ wants you." That night Richard came forward and found new life in Christ.

These young people longed for something of their own, something personal, something genuinely satisfying. In alcohol and riotous living, they found only temporary, momentary highs, not satisfying and lasting peace. But now they had begun to know what real living was all about.

7

Street Meetings and College

After camp was over, I became involved in street meetings. A minister from another church group was holding street services and I knew several young people who were involved in this type of ministry. I attended a service, not participating, but one of the young ladies who sang in a trio recognized me. Knowing I was a Christian and of my past, she invited me to the next meeting to give my testimony.

This was not to my liking because I knew how some of these meetings ended—speakers splattered with eggs or mocked and cursed. I felt people would think I was some kind of holy roller if I preached on the street corner. Before my conversion I thought the same thing, I recalled.

One time, coming from uptown New York after taking a fix, my friends and I walked to Forty-Second Street and Times Square where the street evangelists were. We laughed at one and mocked her, not really knowing what she was talking about. I felt that if I participated in street meetings I would get the same treatment. But seeing these young Christians give themselves in this way, I thought, *If they can stand the jeering and mocking, I certainly can.*

That whole week I was nervous, constantly thinking about Friday night when the street meeting was supposed to take place. The meeting was to be held in my own home area, Flushing, in Queens, on the main artery. I knew some of my old associates would see me. I wondered: would they laugh at me or be sympathetic toward the cause of Christ?

My mother, knowing I planned to participate, advised me not to go. She thought a fight might break out and she didn't want me involved with anything like that anymore. I took assurance from the words of Paul that, "for me to live is Christ, to die is gain." However, I knew it wasn't going to be that severe. Nevertheless, I felt very tense, because I thought I would be facing a lot of people I knew and giving my testimony to people who did not understand what the gospel is all about. I had no idea what their reaction would be.

Taking my Bible, I went to the designated spot. All the young people who had participated in the meeting the previous week were there with the street evangelist. Before the service, all the participants met off to one side and prayed. Suddenly, as though Christ himself were right in the midst of our group, I knew he was going to guide us that night.

At eight o'clock we started the service. We had a police permit, an American flag, the Christian flag, and a portable platform. To start the service, Mr. Gallo, the street evangelist, spoke out, reading from the Bible, and preaching very loudly. Soon we had a good-sized gathering and were off to a fine start. After Brother Gallo finished, his daughter and another girl mounted the platform to sing.

When young men passing by saw these two fine looking girls get up to sing, they were attracted and stopped to see what was going on. More people gathered until we had a large crowd of young people. After the special song, Mr. Gallo thought it would be a good time for me to give my testimony.

I told the group how the Lord delivered me from a terrible life of sin, from drug addiction, but apparently people didn't believe it. I could tell by the expressions on their faces they weren't going for it. I could almost read their thoughts: *Nobody is powerful enough to deliver a guy from drug addiction when he is using heroin.* A number of young people turned their backs to me, shook their heads, and gave the wave-off, as though I were speaking through my hat. They were not going to buy it. Yet, a sizable group kept listening.

After I finished, Mr. Gallo again rose to speak, the girls sang another song, and an invitation was given. Three or four people came forward that night, one a young fellow in his early twenties. Brother Gallo came to me and said, "Vince, this young man was quite taken by what you had to say."

I walked over to him and asked him if he was a Christian. He said no. I asked, "What made you stay and listen to the rest of the service?"

He replied, "Tonight I'm supposed to be with my gang. We planned to pull a job on a gas station. For some reason I came past here and heard you speak. I thought it would be better for me to stay and listen than to go along with my gang to the holdup." This young man gave his heart to the Lord that night. I participated in several more of these street meetings and had wonderful experiences, a little nerve-racking at times, but spiritually rewarding.

As summer drew to an end, I continued to prepare for college. After I had felt God's call on my life, I sought counsel from people who I felt could give me sound advice about entering college. Not having a high school diploma, I knew there were going to be some bumps in the road. I thought, too, perhaps I couldn't enter a college until I received my high school diploma. Nevertheless, I inquired about it.

I learned of a small Bible college in Camrose, Alberta, Canada, about sixty miles southeast of Edmonton. It was in a town primarily agricultural, with a population of around seven thousand. In response to my letter requesting admission, I received from the dean of admissions an acceptance on the condition that I would be placed on academic probation.

Early in September I said good-bye to friends and relatives, was driven to Kennedy Airport by my mother and sister, and departed for Ontario by plane.

At customs I was asked why I was going to Canada. I replied that I was going to college. "Where is your letter of acceptance?" the officer asked. My mind froze for a moment as I realized I had left the letter at home. One of the guards said, "How do I know for sure you're going to a Bible college in Camrose? You could be a smuggler!"

I took my Bible out of my valise and showed it to him, all the while explaining my intention to study for the ministry. After a short period of uncertainty, the guards gave me a four-day permit, explaining that I had to get another permit from the immigration agent in Edmonton. I breathed a big sigh of relief. At that moment I heard my flight number called.

I boarded a trans-Canadian super jet and soared off toward Edmonton, Alberta, about three and one-half hours away. During that whole flight I was deep in prayer, asking God to strengthen my mind, to give me the discipline I needed for studying at college. I was one scared, frightened individual. Upon arriving at the Edmonton airport I immediately felt a difference in the climate. The air was much drier and a very low overcast made it a rather gloomy day.

Upon inquiring, I learned that Camrose was about sixty-five miles from the airport. No buses ran at that time of night, but I was told I could spent the night at a hotel and take a train out the next morning. Eager to get to the school and see what it was like, I took a bus into Edmonton and from there hired a cab.

The driver said he normally could not make the long run to Camrose. He would take me out this time for a certain amount of money. Since the Canadian exchange had brought me back more money than I had had, I figured the ride would be on the Canadian government. So this young cab driver drove me to Camrose.

Arriving at the school, I found to my surprise it was smaller than I had thought it would be. I reminded myself that it was a place of learning, that my primary objective was to learn more about Jesus Christ, to better prepare myself for his work. I entered a deserted vestibule at the main building, then rang the front doorbell. When there was no response, I walked in.

A group of girls scattered in all directions, I thought, like chickens without heads. One of the girls told the dean of women I was downstairs so she came and welcomed me to the school. I was told to take my luggage to the rear of the building and across the courtyard to the boys' dormitory.

The first person I met upon entering the boys' dormitory was Mr. Paul Kilburn, a professor who was to become a dear friend. He introduced me to other students. My roommate was a young fellow, Cleve Unger, also to become a cherished friend.

Later, while I unpacked, questions were thrown at me. The boys learned I was from a big city, and they asked me all about it. I gave them only brief answers, I was so tired and weary from my trip. After devotions,

I dropped my head on the pillow, tried to sort out my confused thoughts, and, before I knew it, dozed off, sleeping soundly until morning.

That day I went shopping with Cleve and another boy, Eric. Giving Camrose the once-over, I thought to myself, *Man, I've seen some small places before, but this one takes the cake. If you were driving and happened to sneeze, you'd miss the whole thing.* Seriously, it was a nice town with friendly people.

As we walked around Camrose, I was amazed to see guys wearing cowboy hats. I thought this type of getup was just for the movies, so I asked if this was for real or if there was something special going on—like a rodeo. Cleve, who was from the area, said the people dressed that way all the time. I felt kind of lost and out-of-place, so after about an hour of sightseeing we returned to the school.

With three days before classes were to start, I decided to look the school over beforehand. I walked through the building, looking at classrooms, then went into the library with another student. On the library wall hung pictures of students who had previously attended. As I looked over the pictures I noticed one girl and asked, "What about her? Is she still a student?"

My friend said, "Yes, she was a student last year but I don't think she will be coming back this year."

I thought to myself, *too bad!* She was nice looking and perhaps nice to be with. Still, I reminded myself that I was there to learn. For the next two days I stayed to myself, still tense and a bit nervous about starting classes. One of the boys had a football and occasionally I tossed the pigskin around, but I couldn't keep my mind off my concern about school. I felt sure that the Lord was going to watch over me, but still there were unanswered questions in my mind.

The day classes started I awakened extra early. I felt I needed all the spiritual strength I could get through prayer. That first day of orientation we met Dean Wiuff, President Irving, and the rest of the staff and faculty. That day seemed pleasant and easy enough and I calmed down a bit. Certain terms used in our orientation were foreign to me, so I jotted them down and later asked another student what they meant. I wanted to learn all I possibly could.

That afternoon I was called into Dean Wiuff's office where he and I had a long talk. He was an American, I learned, so we had something in common. He expressed concern over my background. Referring to a transcript of my grades from the high school I attended in New York City, he noted that I was not an ideal student. He said it was his duty to warn me that school was going to be rough.

He again stressed the fact that I was being placed on probation, explaining this meant I would have to maintain a C average in order to continue my studies at the college. I told him I would do my best to adjust to school policy and would work hard at my studies. After he prayed with me, I returned to my room.

The first few days of classes involved the introduction to each subject I was going to take, so there was no homework or collateral reading assigned. I was ready, though, when Saturday came. I found that was the time to do laundry, ironing, room cleaning.

On Saturday, two other fellows and I were sitting in the students' lounge when a pretty girl, a stranger to me, strolled in. With a jolt I realized she was the young lady whose picture I had seen hanging in the school library. Jabbing one of my friends with an elbow, I said, "I thought you said she wasn't coming back." He shrugged his shoulders, not knowing why she had come back. Little did I know that the girl I was looking at was the one I would marry.

I wasted no time in meeting Ruth Beach, hoping we would strike up a friendship. However, we soon found we had a personality clash—I didn't particularly care for her personality and she didn't dig mine, either.

Classes were soon in full swing and I was in the thick of studies and really confused. The old truism "Too much too soon" hit me like an avalanche. Assignments piled up, too much for me to take. I tried my best, rising each morning at five o'clock to read two hours before classes. During lunch hour I gulped my food, then rushed to the library.

Realizing I had too heavy a load, I went to the dean and asked if he thought I should drop a couple of courses. We decided I should drop two subjects, making the burden much lighter, but it was still difficult for me to maintain a C average. In fact, that first marking period I had a D average. The school was really lenient with me and gave me a second chance.

One of the most difficult subjects for me was English. I needed extra help with this, so Professor Ivan Dinsmore volunteered to help me at night. The help he gave me really helped my college work.

The classes were interesting; however, I lacked something which I just could not pinpoint. I talked to my advisor about my lack of ability to comprehend what was said in class. For the few weeks I had been at

Alberta Bible Institute I hadn't gotten above fifty-nine on any of my tests and I couldn't understand why I was doing so poorly. I had done my homework, completed my outside reading, followed my syllabus to the letter. Yet, no results. I told Mr. Kilburn I thought maybe my coming to A.B.I. was a mistake.

He asked me how long I had been out of school. I told him nine or ten years, but that I was never a good student to begin with. I told him I was expelled from high school. He advised me to spend this first year getting oriented, learning to discipline myself, getting accustomed to being a student.

However, I felt that God hadn't brought me out to Alberta—three thousand miles from home—just to become disciplined. Of course, it was excellent advice, as many educators say when I tell them this story. I simply knew how I felt at that time, being the oldest student in the college and feeling like the dumbest— although I can laugh about it now.

I felt very inferior to those young people who were my schoolmates. Here they were reaching grades of eighty and ninety, while I was struggling to hold a D average. Feeling bad about this, I found it hard to look faculty members and students in the eye.

After my talk with Mr. Kilburn, however, I decided it was time to clash with God. I did not think this was disrespectful; I simply had to talk to the Lord and I needed some answers. I didn't mean to be abrupt in what I said, but this situation was a do-or-die matter— like an all-or-nothing play in a basketball or hockey game. My whole future, I felt, rested upon what I could accomplish and make of myself while at A.B.I.

I went back to my room, locked the door, dropped to my knees, and prayed. I waited for an answer, prayed again, and waited some more. After an hour I decided to get off my knees and get to my textbooks and really do some severe and rigid studying. Although I studied three hours a day prior to the time I had talked with the Lord, nothing was sinking in. I felt I needed to study more. I began to study seven to nine hours a day, aside from classwork. And did it work!

We had a Personal Evangelism examination and I made a perfect score. Then we had a Bible Survey exam and I got a passing grade. My grades in all my subjects began to climb. I counted it nothing less than a miracle from God. Yes, I studied and applied myself, but I believe God miraculously gave me the desire to discipline myself so I would be able to sit for great lengths of time reading and studying.

When the second marking period came around I went from a D average up to a C average. The wife of one of my professors congratulated me. When she heard I had gotten a perfect score on my Personal Evangelism test she was especially happy because her husband, Professor Yamabe, was teaching this class. Of course, when she congratulated me, I walked into the main building with my head in the clouds. I really felt good. The rest of the students, who had been praying and pulling for me, rejoiced with me.

My social life was not very sociable because I spent most of my time studying. However, one day I played in a student-faculty football game. I looked forward to this game, thinking it might be good for me to work out some of my frustrations on the field. It was a very interesting game. However, I didn't think the physical contact was going to be as rough as it was.

On one of the plays the teachers had the ball and Dean Wiuff charged through the line. Catching me completely off guard, he knocked me for a loop. It also flattened my ego because a number of faculty wives and other students were watching the game and cheering us on. I thought to myself, *Well, if you want it that way, two can play that game.*

Again, the teachers had the ball. At the signal, "hike," I tore into their line and smashed Dean Wiuff. The next thing I knew he was on the ground. He slowly got to his feet. Then, holding his back, he said, "My back, my back," and awkwardly shuffled off the field. I felt bad because I had put him out of the game, but of course he took it in stride. The ovation I received from the student body served to pump up my ego.

The only other time I associated with other students was when we cleaned up after dinner, washed dishes, or cleaned potatoes. During these times we joked around and sang songs. Often, in my spare time, I would walk and meditate. Nobody was forced to read his Bible or pray. It was taken for granted that each student would have his own devotions. During that year I drew closer to God and my faith increased.

One night while walking I saw one of the women students leave the dormitory. It was about eight o'clock and quite dark out, so I asked her where she was going. Then I recognized Ruth, the girl whose picture I'd admired. She said she had a Christian Education assignment that had to be done for the next day—she had to interview two primaries to see what they thought God looked like, who he was, where he lived.

It sounded like fun so I asked her if I could join her. We began to walk and talk. She asked me about New York and I asked her about Ontario. I found out she wasn't a farm-type girl, but one with whom I could discuss scholastic matters.

Ruth soon found two young primaries to interview. One said, "God has red hair and a long red beard."

The other one said, "No, God has a long black beard and black hair." When she asked them where he lived, simultaneously one pointed up and the other down. We got a big laugh out of this. The temperature, well below zero, made it impossible to stay out for more than a half-hour or so.

Going back to the school, Ruth and I had hot chocolate and shared our hopes and visions. Ruth's father had served as a missionary in India for about four years. While there he became very ill and had to return to Ontario to convalesce. Ruth felt she would like to go back to India to work with orphans. She had been offered a position with a women's missionary society.

I told her I had thought of becoming an evangelist, working with young people, because my past experience appealed to youth.

From that evening, Ruth and I became good friends. We began to take walks together during the afternoon and became better acquainted. Several weeks passed and, although we did not spend any great amount of time together, I found myself falling in love with her.

One day I walked into my room and said to my roommate, "I'm going to marry that girl."

He just about cracked up laughing, and said, "You American guys are fast! The same thing happened to my sister."

One Sunday evening in church I was sitting about two rows behind Ruth, and as I looked at her I noticed a cross over her head! Now, on the walls of the church in Camrose are grooves painted gold. They run horizontally and vertically. Just where Ruth was sitting, there appeared to be a cross right above her head. I marveled at this and took this as a sign that Ruth was the girl the Lord had for me.

While we walked one day I expressed my feelings to Ruth and she said she felt the same way. I asked her if she would accept an engagement ring from me and she answered yes. Just before Christmas a small package arrived from the States. I gave Ruth her diamond, and we were engaged.

However, this caused some controversy in the college. Their policy was that no student could become engaged during the school year. I had neglected to read that part in the Student Handbook, not thinking I would get engaged or even go steady with anyone. At first I was quite hesitant about taking the ring back. But I saw I was wrong, so we canceled our engagement.

I felt that Ruth was a great asset to me in my studies and I think I even helped her in hers. My grades rose above a C average and Ruth was keeping her grades up so we were not slack in our scholastic lives. She and I often met for prayer. Once, the faculty thought Ruth and I were seeing too much of each other. We learned of this toward the latter part of the first semester, and decided not to see each other so often during the second semester.

Christmas came and I decided to stay in Canada. I was invited to stay at the home of Ruth's sister who lived at Biggar, Saskatchewan. I had a most enjoyable time there. It was very cold, plunging to nearly fifty degrees below zero. We went out every day to feed the livestock. It was so cold that the electric pump, used to pump water for the animals, froze and broke.

We had to haul the water up with buckets on long ropes. As soon as the water was poured from the buckets into the trough, it crusted over with ice. I kidded Ruth's family about the deep cold by saying water soaked inside my glove and before I could jerk my glove off and wipe away the water, there was a little ice cube in my hand!

8

Marriage and Ministry

Although Christmas vacation was most delightful, I was eager for school to start again. I wanted to get the first semester over with. Soon, studies again began in earnest. Ruth and I saw very little of each other. I took the engagement ring back, but we both knew God had plans for our lives together.

It was not necessary for me to see Ruth every day—I knew she loved me and I loved her. During the second semester she had seventeen credits to obtain in order to graduate that year. Of course, I struggled to keep up with a thirteen-hour schedule. Nevertheless, that year with God's help I disciplined myself. When it came time for finals, I was sure I would succeed.

A.B.I. offered young Christians a varied ministry. Students went to nursing homes, or to the big hospital, during special times of the year—Christmas, Thanksgiving—as well as during the school year. We distributed tracts, religious literature, and just shared with them what Christ meant to our lives. At Christmas we went through the halls of the hospital singing Christmas carols. We wished patients happy season's greetings, and prayed God's richest blessing upon them. I was encouraged to think that we could inspire those in need.

One girl at a nursing home had a very strange disease. Her muscles were tightening up, so she had no flexibility in her arms or legs. However, I visited Rita on several occasions during the year. I found that, instead of my being a comfort to her, she was a great inspiration to me. We students prayed often for her healing, always desiring that God's will be done.

At the end of the semester Ruth graduated. We were catapulted into summer vacation. The night of her graduation Ruth's sister, Lavonne, and brother-in-law, Ken, took us to the Edmonton airport. Good-byes were not easy, but finally accomplished when our flight for Toronto was called. Of course, I planned to return that September to A.B.I. While Ruth and I were flying toward Toronto, I thought of postponing our engagement for awhile to see if our love was real. When I told Ruth this, she was hurt by it. I explained I would rather be sure when I gave her the ring again. She said she understood this.

When we landed at Toronto, Ruth's parents, her brother, and sister-in-law were waiting for us. I was very eager to meet them since I had heard so much about them. And they wanted to see who their Ruth had been engaged to.

We had a brief wait at the airport before my plane jetted off to New York City, where my mother and sister would meet me. For some reason, as I said good-bye to Ruth, I thought that would be the last time I would see her. Yet, when I boarded the New York-bound plane I felt as if part of me were still in Canada. I had had a similar feeling when my cousin Jackie died. It seemed that a little bit of me died with him. That plane ride home was not enjoyable. Each mile farther from Ruth deepened the misery inside me. I realized I had left behind the only person I had ever really loved. Still, I had to be sure. I felt that marriage was a very sacred thing, not a toy.

When I arrived at Kennedy Airport, my mother and Rose Marie were there to greet me. It wasn't a completely happy reunion, though, because I felt sick inside that I had left in Canada the girl I loved.

When I got home I asked about my relatives and made small talk for awhile. Then I decided to visit Mrs. Bowser. When I arrived at her house, Margo, her granddaughter was there. I was glad to see both of them. We visited happily for awhile. Then Margo and I had a long talk and I found that all I could talk about was Ruth.

When I left their house I knew beyond all doubt Ruth was the one God had for me. Without hesitation I called Ruth in Canada. At first she didn't recognize my voice! My call really surprised her. I asked her, "Will you accept my ring and become my wife?"

Her reply was a question, "Vince, are you sure this is what you really want to do?"

I said, "Yes, I am completely certain." Two weeks later, I flew to Canada and gave Ruth the engagement ring. At first, because of school policy we planned to wait a year to be married. But after counseling with several people, including my prospective father-in-law, we decided to marry that summer. We learned there was a good evangelical college in Kitchener, Ontario—Emmanuel Bible College. I wrote a letter requesting permission to enroll. A return letter stated I had been accepted on a conditional status so Ruth and I set our wedding date: August 13, 1966.

Back in the States, I began to seek employment and finally got a job driving airport limousines. However, the pay wasn't adequate and I didn't particularly like the job. One day I went down to the Meat Cutters Union in Manhattan. While there I spoke to the union delegate, knowing that since I had no experience lugging meat down on the docks, the chances of my getting a job were less than slim.

The man told me to sit in the hall and wait, in case something might come in. The union delegate came out of his office, looked around for someone, then returned to his office. A bit later he came out again, looked for someone, turned, and went back inside. I silently prayed, *Dear Lord, if he doesn't call me to go to work the next time he comes out of his office, I'm leaving.*

The next time the union delegate came out, he looked around, started back into his office, then turned around and said, "Hey, you there! Kid, come here!" He gave me an address to go to for work and I worked there all summer, making, along with Ruth's earnings, sufficient money for college.

My parents had not met Ruth, so we asked her parents if she could come to New York and spend the weekend with my family. Permission was given, so Ruth came to the city and met my family. When they all met her, they loved her, and really accepted her as one of the family.

August 13 came around before we knew it. Although I was tense and nervous I could hardly wait for the wedding ceremony to take place. Ruth was radiantly beautiful. The ceremony was lovely and meaningful, and afterward we had a delicious dinner, served by the women's group of the Welland, Ontario congregation, the church my father-in-law pastored.

Later that day, my parents, my best friend, and Rose Marie, needed a ride back to the Buffalo airport. Ruth and I volunteered to take them back. Without my knowledge, a couple of fellows had decorated my car. Signs reading JUST MARRIED were plastered all over it. The six of us piled into the car and headed for the airport. On the way we had to go through customs. As I pulled up to the immigration booth I told the officer I had just gotten married. Eyeing the signs on the car, he responded, "I gathered that." Then he looked into the car, stepped back with a look of shock and said, "Don't tell me they're all going on the honeymoon with you!" We told him what had happened and why we were going to the airport, so he waved us through.

After our honeymoon week in Toronto, we went to Kitchener, where our apartment was located about a mile from Emmanuel Bible College. A fine Christian man had found a three and one-half room apartment that was just what we wanted and was also within our means. There we spent two very happy years. My time at Emmanuel Bible College was deeply rewarding. I had difficulty with some of my subjects, but through the discipline I had developed at A.B.I., I was able to study and get good grades. When I first started college I had a D average; when I graduated I had a B+ average. This was possible because of good friends who took time to help me with philosophy, theology, and other subjects. I profited greatly from my studies and learned to apply their principles to needs in people's lives.

Ruth applied for work and had several interviews, each of which caused her to say, "Oh, I wish I wouldn't have to work there because of the environment." Or, "It seemed like such a dull position." Then she learned of an opening at a Canadian subsidiary of an American firm. Before she went to Sprout Waldron for her interview, we both prayed asking the Lord to open a door. We asked him to provide work for Ruth in a suitable atmosphere.

I drove Ruth to her appointment in Waterloo, about two miles from Kitchener. She got out of the car, went for the interview, and was gone a long time. Finally, she came down, her wide smile broadcasting her success. She got in the car and said, "Oh, honey, you will never guess what. My future boss is a Christian! And did we ever have a good talk. We talked about you mainly." Already surprised, I could hardly believe her when Ruth said, "Come on up. He wants to meet you."

I went upstairs and met Ruth's employer, Mr. Ed Wertman. This man was a tremendous inspiration to us, and on occasions Mr. Wertman felt led of the Lord to give us financial aid. Many times we had fellowship with him and his wife. God really blessed us in Kitchener.

While I was attending E.B.C. word spread that the college had a former drug addict who was now studying for the ministry. People wanted to hear a drug addict tell about his experiences, describe what it was like to live in New York City. Calls began to come to the college for me to speak. However I did not want to become a church gypsy. I wanted to stay at one church to learn how a local congregation works. Although I was attending college for this, I knew there is nothing like practical experience.

However, I did have a message to tell, and it was very difficult for me to deny the calls. So I began to accept invitations to go to various churches to preach. I had been teaching a Sunday school class of juniors, and disliked having to give it up. However, it seemed God opened the door for me to experience a wider ministry. Within a few months I had spoken to Mennonites, Baptists, United Missionary groups, Pentecostal churches. I served at youth rallies and in rescue missions.

One of the most interesting experiences I had in outside preaching came about ten o'clock one night after Ruth and I had just returned home from a meeting. I answered the jangling phone and heard a woman's voice say, "Hello, Vince?"

I said, "Yes. Speaking."

She said, "I thought you were supposed to preach for us tonight." I did not know what she was talking about. She said I had made an appointment with her husband for that very night, to speak at a Mennonite campground. Somehow our dates had gotten mixed up. I thought it was next Sunday.

I said, "My appointment is not until next week."

She insisted, "It is for tonight. We have over one hundred families out here waiting to hear you speak."

I asked, "Where are you?" She named a place called Hidden Acres, about forty miles away. She hurriedly gave me directions.

I turned from the phone and told Ruth I had a speaking engagement that night. Ruth looked at me and said, "Oh, no. You're kidding!"

I said, "No, come on. Let's go!" We got into our car and headed in the direction of Hidden Acres. The road was strange to me. I had to make turns that were hard to see. We were going as fast as eighty-five miles an hour. Both Ruth and I prayed for safety—for ourselves and others we met.

After about a half-hour we met a car near a side road, the clue my caller had indicated we should watch for. We swung off the highway and jolted after the car along a side road for about a mile. Deep in a thick woods we finally came to a big clearing. I told Ruth, "They have the right name for this place—Hidden Acres."

As we parked, I saw two men on a hay wagon, spotlights pointing toward them while they played a guitar and a violin. They looked at me and both gave one big sigh, as if to say "Thank goodness you have arrived." I learned they had played the whole evening waiting for me to get there. The man playing the guitar had blisters on his fingers.

I thought of John Wesley as I left my car, climbed atop a picnic table, then jumped onto the hay wagon. With no time to prepare I just used John 3:1-7 for my text after the man with whom I had made the appointment introduced me. I preached to some one hundred families, giving them the message which I felt God inspired in me. After I concluded a number of young people came forward to inquire about the Lord.

Another time I preached to a congregation of about three hundred. At the end of the service an invitation was given to any present who might need spiritual help. Several young people and a middle-aged woman came forward and knelt, crying, burdened. The woman said to her pastor, "You know me as a Christian, but I want to confess something. The man I am living with is not my husband. I have been living as a common-law wife for five years. I cannot live with myself unless Christ forgives me and helps me straighten up my life."

She asked the pastor to call me over to where she and the pastor were. She thanked me for my honest message, then told me her predicament. After we had prayed, this woman went away with renewed faith in God. She had found power and motivation to break out of her dilemma.

One couple Ruth and I grew to love in Kitchener was Denzil and Iris Baker. A young Anglo-Indian pastor, Denzil met lovely Iris while she was a missionary in India. Ruth also had known Iris in India. A tremendous influence on his people in India, Denzil had come to Canada to do further work in theology and to complete his college work. Many times Denzil and I went for walks and talked about spiritual matters. We had great fun times too.

Ruth and I invited Denzil and Iris to our apartment for a spaghetti dinner. Denzil had a difficult time eating spaghetti Italian style with a spoon and fork. He tried to pick up the elusive spaghetti, but only succeeded in getting spaghetti sauce all over himself. He finally made the sober statement, "My dentist told me not to eat too much food because I have a sore jawbone."

What was perhaps my greatest thrill came when, along with two other students, I was asked to represent our graduating class. We were asked to give from five- to ten-minute speeches, expressing our feelings about the college. I knew it was a great honor to be asked to speak to such a fine audience. About thirteen hundred persons attended our graduation ceremony.

My mouth became dust-dry as I waited to give my speech. When my turn came to go to the podium and give my address, I became so nervous I lost my vision for a couple of seconds. Then I mumbled and stammered around to find words, although I had a full manuscript in front of me. I felt so many eyes peering at me I wanted to disappear. But once I began to speak, I sensed God's calming presence and spoke passably well.

For two or three months before my graduation, Ruth and I were concerned about where we would serve the Lord. We had earnestly prayed concerning this. We wanted to go anyplace where God wanted us, and felt he had a specific place for us to go.

One evening I received a phone call from Pastor Robert Clock, the man who preached the day I received Jesus Christ. He said, "Vinnie, what are you going to do after you graduate?" I told him I had been praying about it and was thinking of working with youth in a church in New Jersey. Then I asked him why his interest. He told me about a church in Rensselaer, New York, about three miles from Albany. "The church," he said, "needs a pastor, and needs one badly." He gave me the name of the contact person in case I was interested.

I contacted Mr. Geraldson who told us the congregation was in a sad state, that it would require a lot of work to build it up. He said he felt it could be done if the right pastor came. I had once preached at that church, I recalled, and knew it had a number of pastors within a short time. In fact, my friend, Ken Crouch, had once pastored the church. After being told the church was in need spiritually and financially, Ruth and I were invited to visit with the people and conduct a worship service. Mr. Geraldson said, "Vince, you can count on about fifteen people showing up for the service."

Personally, I did not care how many might attend the service. But I was concerned about how many people would be interested in building the congregation again, and if they were seriously concerned about the cause of Christ. Since the church had been some time without a pastor, a number of parishioners had drifted to other churches.

The Saturday evening we arrived for our visit a business meeting was held. It was rewarding when I asked what would be my limitation as their pastor and the people said they would give me a free hand. I could do anything I thought was right to do in that area, since I had come from New York City, not too far away. During the business meeting I learned the church had a bank balance of about eighty dollars, and that very few people attended services there anymore.

We planned a service for the next day. I was quite nervous, yet I felt that God was opening a door for us to minister to those people. In the morning we neglected to open the church door early enough to let the organist in. Finding the doors locked she thought there was to be no service, so she returned home.

Right after that people started arriving and it was soon worship time, eleven o'clock. Since we had no organist, we just sang a cappella. However, I was thrilled by the attendance. Several of the young people in that area were there—ones I'd met at youth camp some years before. There were about fifteen or twenty in attendance, certainly an answer to prayer because we were expecting eight or nine. I sensed God's very presence during the entire service. I felt this was where I belonged and I felt quite at home, not nervous at all. The experience I'd had preaching while in Bible college really made a difference for me.

After the morning service we were asked out to eat, but Ruth and I felt we should be alone to talk and evaluate the situation. At dinner, Ruth looked rather strangely at me and I stared at her. Finally, I blurted out, "Honey, I feel this is where God wants us to serve." Taking a deep breath, I swallowed and said, "Let's face it. This church is so far gone now that if we did anything wrong we couldn't hurt it."

We went back to Canada and continued to search the Lord's will. We continued to correspond with the board of trustees of the church in Rensselaer. Reports indicated there was a renewal of spirit and the people were looking forward to our coming. This encouraged me as I counseled with my father-in-law about the advisability of going to Rensselaer. After we prayed, he said he felt it would be good for us to go down. Although it was a small congregation, it would provide good training for Ruth and me.

Ruth and I decided to accept the challenge and moved to Rensselaer. When we arrived we were greeted by some of the young people and Harriet and Irma Hammond, two wonderful individuals who have supported the church for years. The church and house were run-down and broken glass was strewn around the property. The first thing Ruth and I did was to call a workday. We invited all the young people in the area, Catholic, Jews, whoever wanted to come and help us clean up the church property.

We got a wonderful response. Kids came with lawn mowers and rakes. On such a large lot it was a tough job, but all seemed eager to help. At the first Sunday morning church service we had only eleven people in attendance. But after doing a little neighborhood calling, we started seeing results. From the eleven people we started with, the church in Rensselaer was averaging forty-five in attendance within a year and a half.

People had told us we would be working in a very difficult area, that we couldn't expect genuine conversions, that people would be hypocritical. But time and again, older youths and adults came to the altar and yielded their lives to the Lord. They broke down and cried, deeply repentant over their sins. I wasn't pushing for emotional conversion. I only wanted people to acknowledge that Jesus Christ is the Son of God and the only hope for salvation. I yearned for people to hear and understand this message, because this is the message that changed my life and burned in my heart.

9

And Jackie Makes Three

In mid-October 1968 Ruth told me she thought we were going to become parents. Well, I found that rather hard to believe because we had had previous disappointments. But she was almost positive this time. So I drove her to the doctor's office. While in the waiting room, I could not take my eyes off her. I pretended to look through a *Life* magazine, but kept one eye on her. After several minutes of waiting, Ruth was called into the doctor's examination room.

I settled impatiently to wait. That twenty-minute wait seemed more like twenty hours. I thought I would burst wondering whether or not we were going to have a little one. My thoughts wandered back over my past life as a junkie. I'd heard of babies being born deformed, so this was a great concern of mine. In a way, I hoped Ruth was mistaken, preferring this to the baby's not being normal in some way.

After what seemed ages, Ruth came out, her face flushed. Giving me her widest smile, she winked. My heart thudded as fear left me and I felt that everything was going to be all right and I was very happy. Then the doctor came out and said, "Yes, she's pregnant." He looked at me in a peculiar way, then said, "That'll be seven dollars."

Still in a bit of shock, I finally realized I was going to be a father. I said, "I don't care if you charge me seventy dollars." Later I realized I hadn't known what I was saying.

Apparently the doctor thought I didn't want a baby because he now looked at me and said, "You want the baby, don't you?"

I said, "Of course, we both do!"

He said, "Well, that's a relief to my mind. When I looked at you, you looked as though you didn't want your wife to have a baby."

We wanted the child all right. It was approximately three years since our marriage, and Ruth and I had hoped to start a family after two years of marriage.

Of course, after we learned the good news, we went straight home and made calls to Canada and to New York to tell our parents. They were thrilled to hear we were going to have a little one. I think my parents were a bit more excited, because it was going to be their first grandchild while Ruth's parents were grandparents five times over.

Ruth's health was good; she had very little sickness. Things went just according to plans for nine months. But then things went off schedule — one week, then two weeks, five extra weeks dragged by, and still no baby. The doctor was rather concerned about it and said we'd give it another three or four days and if the baby delayed, he would act. Ruth was starting to become upset and I still worried about whether the child would be affected by my past use of drugs. We finally resorted to prayer, putting it all in God's care.

On Sunday, May 25, 1969, we were to have a guest speaker at our church. Missionary Harry Nachtigall was scheduled to share with us what was happening in Kenya, Africa. While I made preparations for the morning service, Ruth came to me and said, "Vince, I feel funny inside."

Incredulous, I said, "Not this morning. Not Sunday morning! Harry is coming and there's going to be a church full of people out there."

She looked at me and said, "Well, honey, I can't help it."

"Look, Ruth," I said, "you're probably imagining these things."

"No, I'm not!" she insisted. I told her to go inside and lie down. She did, but a few minutes later she said, "Vince, the pains are every fifteen minutes."

I thought to myself, *Oh, no! This just can't be!* Aloud I said, "You'd better call the doctor."

The doctor told her to wait until the pains came every ten minutes. Then she should leave for the hospital. Ruth went back into the bedroom and started packing. Fortunately, in our congregation was a registered nurse, Mrs. Louise Tozer, who sat with Ruth until the contractions were ten minutes apart.

Ruth said, "Vince, we'd better leave pretty soon." But Harry Nachtigall had not yet arrived. Knowing he'd never been in our area before, I didn't want him to come in without knowing what was going on. As Ruth and I were about to walk out the door, a Ford bearing Indiana license plates pulled into our driveway. Harry was driving.

When he walked into the house, I handed him the order of the worship service, introduced ourselves and said, "Excuse me, but my wife is having a baby and we have to go to the hospital now." After we had a few brief words in the kitchen, I excitedly walked out of the house, got into the car and started out of the driveway.

Suddenly I heard Mr. Nachtigall yell, "You'd better wait for your wife!" Ruth wasn't even in the car with me. Everybody could tell I wasn't too excited!

Our ride to the hospital was uneventful. I didn't drive fast because it was a very bumpy road but neither did I stop for any red lights! By the time we arrived at the hospital Ruth's contractions were every three minutes. Nurses took her up to the labor room and told me I could stay there with her. I stayed with Ruth for about two hours. But, remembering we had planned to have seventeen people at our house as guests that day, I told Ruth I would go home for awhile, check on our guests, and find out how the service had gone.

We lived about ten minutes from the hospital, so I hurried home in time to see that our guests had made themselves at home and prepared their own dinner. There was no need for me to stay there any longer so I went back to the hospital. All this time my mind whirled in endless debate over whether the child was going to be normal. I went into the labor room and saw that Ruth was doing fine.

After about twenty minutes Ruth told me to call the doctor. An intern came in, examined her, and said it was almost time. He wheeled her off to the delivery room.

Steve Miller, one of the young men from our church, had come to wait with me, so he and I sat in the waiting room. He was a great comfort to me, telling me how wonderful it was to be a father. He was the father of two fine boys. For hours we waited in the waiting room.

At 8:20 P.M. our doctor walked in and said, "Mr. Guerra?"

I leaped to my feet and said, "Yes, sir?"

He said, "Do you have a big one!"

I gulped and asked, "A big what?"

"A big baby boy! Nine pounds, six ounces."

When he said that I almost fell over. He walked away with obvious pride and a spring in his step. I was speechless. But as soon as I regained my senses I called Ruth's parents in Canada and mine in New York City. Of course there was great rejoicing.

While I was talking to my mother, the nurse brought Jackie, my son, to me. I stared at him, although I was almost too frightened to look. I couldn't get over the size of him, especially the size of his hands! I asked the nurse how his reflexes were.

She said, "He's perfect in every way."

Inexpressible happiness and joy welled up inside me and I silently praised my great Lord for giving us such a fine, healthy, strapping son.

10

Divine Appointment

In spite of the success we experienced with Prospect Heights church, I felt restless. In June 1969, after serving the Rensselaer church for a year and a half, Ruth and I attended an international convention in Indiana. While there I talked to an experienced minister, sharing with him my feeling of restlessness. He, in turn, shared with me an experience he had when he was a young pastor. Then he gave me this advice: "Just be patient. Hold on and you will see the Lord's will. Don't make any snap decisions."

After that conversation I talked to an evangelist who was also a good friend. After I told him about my restlessness, he said, "Well, Vince, God may be preparing you for something big or for some other work." He prayed with me and advised me to just keep open to God's will.

Soon after our arrival, my mother-in-law told me about a Denver Smoot, a minister from Miami, Florida, who worked with drug addicts. It seems he also had a rehabilitation program. Ruth's mother also told me about a young fellow called Seadog, who was with Mr. Smoot. The story was that this boy had very recently become a Christian and was now off drugs. Quite impressed, I wanted to meet this Reverend Smoot, even if only to share my story with him.

Ruth and I stayed in a college dormitory room near the convention center. That evening while Ruth was getting Jackie ready for bed, a knock was heard at the door. I called, "Come in," then stared at the tall, thin-faced, tired-looking man who entered the room. I noticed he had quite long wavy hair, thinning and slightly gray. I thought I knew him, but decided I was wrong.

He spoke in a low voice. "Vincent Guerra?" I nodded yes and he said, "I am Denver Smoot." At my invitation he sat down. I noted his composure, how calm and cool he was about everything. He asked me some questions, about my drug life, my college education, my ministry. After we conversed for awhile, he asked if I would be interested in coming to Miami, Florida to work with drug addicts.

I quickly told him, "No, I don't want to work with drug users. At least, this is not my desire at this time." Even as I spoke, however, there was the nagging thought that while in college and in my more recent ministry, I had felt the urge to minister to users, but had crowded the idea to the back of my mind. I didn't want to get involved in any way with drugs.

Not that I was tempted. I knew that God had given me spiritual power to overcome the temptation to go back to drugs. Even after my conversion I had associated with drug users, had watched them use the needle, smoke marijuana, and not once was I tempted to go back.

I simply felt that the drug ministry would be a complete drag. I knew working with drug addicts could be depressing. When one is rescued there is much rejoicing, true. But converts are few and far between. I said, "Thank you, but I just don't want to get involved in this type of ministry."

Before Mr. Smoot left, he asked me if I would share my experience with a large group of youth, and I quickly agreed. At that meeting I met young Seadog, heard his testimony, and was greatly inspired by it. I, too, shared with the youth. The young people seemed to accept me, if their applause was indication.

Our week at the convention was a spiritual feast for me. I met new friends, heard dynamic messages, sensed the spirit of Christian oneness among thousands of people from around the world.

Ruth and I returned home where our talks often turned to the drug ministry. I asked her what she thought about it, if she was willing to go along with me. Her reply was, "Whatever the Lord wants you to do, that's what I want you to do."

During early summer, I worked with young people at youth camp, but my heart really wasn't in it. I knew some of the kids needed spiritual help, but I felt another minister or layman could easily take my place. A nagging question bothered me: *Who could work with drug addicts?*

I knew from past experience that effective work with addicts required either an ex-drug addict or a very understanding person. When I worked at Teen Challenge, I noticed the addicts listened to the counselors, but they did not really look up to those who knew nothing of the scene or feeling of a drug addict. Some were more attentive when they learned I had gone through difficult periods like theirs.

One day I received a letter from Denver Smoot inviting me to Miami to evaluate his program and approach to the drug ministry. That letter made me upset. I didn't want to leave my church. We were having a tremendous time. People were turning to Christ, the church was growing. Christians were really beginning to witness for the Lord.

My mind clouded with doubt, I went to Mr. Fred Geraldson, a man I deeply admired, showed him the letter, and asked what he thought I should do. He said, "Well, if this is where the Lord wants you he'll make a way for you to go. But if not he'll show in some way that you should stay here in Rensselaer." My board gave permission for me to go to Miami and visit Mr. Smoot.

I flew to Miami and there again met this tall, skinny, tired-looking man. He greeted me warmly, his smile wide and friendly. At once he proceeded to tell me about his work. I marveled at his enthusiasm over the program they had begun. His love and concern for young people were obvious as he poured out his hopes for the drug ministry program. It inspired me to hear a man his age express concern for drug abusers.

That week I met several important people who work with drug addicts in the Miami area. I was permitted to go into the jails with Denver. In the Dade County Jail I had an opportunity to share with convicts there. As I looked at those men I no longer saw their own faces, but the faces of many friends I once had who had taken overdoses, and had died from heroin. I felt I was no longer talking to drug addicts, but to a group of friends who were in need.

To my surprise, these fellows really listened with interest. I thought, If I were in jail and someone came to preach to me about the love of God, after the experience I had had with religion, I would turn him off and go to sleep during his spiel. But these fellows were courteous and seemed to appreciate what I had to say. Seven or eight of the inmates later expressed their personal appreciation.

After I finished, questions came from the group. One question was, "Why should we turn to God now that we're in trouble? Doesn't that seem hypocritical?"

I answered by saying, "When a junkie is on the street and he has a few dollars in his pocket, he doesn't think about God or even care about him. So long as he has buddies and girls and his narcotics, God is the last thought on his mind. But, now in prison, you're perhaps at a place where you're ready and willing to listen to what God has to say to you." He nodded his head and acknowledged my answer.

I told him about a young man I worked with at Guelph Reformatory in Canada. That fellow once declared it was one of the greatest blessings of his life when he was busted. Had he not been caught cracking a safe and been sent to prison, he felt he would never have learned about God and his salvation. Actually he did not "serve time"; he used his time. Of course, he wanted to be released, but while imprisoned he studied to prepare for the time when he was out in the community again. This story seemed to inspire the inmates at Dade County Jail.

A couple of nights later I spoke at the House of Ichthus coffeehouse. This was another first for me. I hesitated to speak at a coffeehouse, knowing that the audiences there can be quite calloused. After praying earnestly about it, I did share with eighty or ninety young people, telling them what Christ had done for me. Their ovation indicated my words were graciously accepted.

While I was in Miami, Mr. Smoot took me to the hip scene psychedelic shops where I met a lot of the hip youth. Many asked me to come back to help some of their friends or even themselves. Many having drug problems wanted to get off drugs, but couldn't find a way out.

It was a great privilege for me to speak in two churches that week I was in Miami. Then, on Tuesday, Reverend Smoot drove me to the airport. I thanked him for the wonderful time he had shown me, boarded my flight, and left Florida. I had no thought of going back to the sunny south. But when I arrived home in New York, Ruth and I talked much about it. She wanted to know what Florida was like, what the houses looked like, if the city was clean, how hot it was. I told her as much as I could remember about the place.

My primary concern, though, was for those drug users. My thoughts went back to the day Denver Smoot drove me to the airport. We had stopped at one of the psychedelic shops. A thirtyish-looking man came over to us. One of the kingpins among the hippie youth, he said, "Fathers (to him, any clergyman not a rabbi was a priest). Fathers, I need help. I want to find meaning in life. I want to find the fifth dimension in life, but not in chemicals or narcotics. I have tried everything and am not satisfied. I need help." We talked, then this man invited Denver to his home.

My mind's eye couldn't turn off that channel even though I soon was back in New York.

Ruth and I had a week's vacation planned, so we rented a trailer about twenty-five miles from our house, in West Sand Lake, New York. Upon meeting the proprietor of the trailer park, I sensed the man was bothered by some burden. I told Ruth what I felt and asked her to pray much about his need.

That vacation was not all fun. Through contacts made by a good friend, Terry Hogue, I had been encouraged to write the story of what had happened in my life—both before and after. That vacation was to be the time I had set aside to do something painful for me—write. Miraculously, I had tools which helped.

Just before our vacation, Ruth and I had visited my sister, Rose Marie, and her husband, Ray, in New York City. Ray asked me how the Lord worked. I told him how God had opened doors for me to go back to school, how he helped Ruth and me in many ways in the ministry and our pastoral work.

We told him about the book we hoped to write and I said, "If I just had a dictaphone, I could dictate into it and Ruth would type up the manuscript."

Ray looked at me and said, "We have in our office seven dictaphones that are not being used. You can use one." I could hardly believe what I heard.

Recovering from my surprise, I said, "See, Ray, apparently the Lord is opening doors so I can write this book. That's how he works."

He looked astonished for a moment, then replied, "Well, Vince, you really have something there."

While Ruth and I vacationed, I worked four hours every morning on my book and we made good progress. However, I prayed God would use me while on vacation to help someone in need.

One afternoon, Mr. Clay, the proprietor of the trailer park, came by. A friendly man from Alabama, he and I started to talk. Soon I told him how the Lord saved my soul. He seemed familiar with the term "saved." I noticed his eyes filled with tears and he seemed to have a hard time swallowing.

He said, "Vince, I have a very bad heart. I don't know if I'm going to live or die in the near future. But then, as I look at some other people I consider myself a very lucky and healthy person." With that he walked away.

I went inside our trailer and told Ruth, "That man is going to be saved before we leave here." We prayed very earnestly for Mr. Clay. That week I read quite a bit, studying the book of Isaiah. Ruth read the book, *Beyond Ourselves,* and tended to little Jackie. We took a few walks, and just enjoyed God's out-of-doors. We threw flat stones into the lake nearby, to see how many times we could make the rocks skip across the surface. We had a relaxing week. And then it was time to return home.

As we were about to leave I said to Ruth, "Let's stop by and see the Clays." We pulled up in front of their luxurious Airstream trailer. Mrs. Clay was working in her flowers. I said, "Mrs. Clay, I want to thank you for everything. We had a wonderful time."

She said, "Vince, before you go, my husband wants to see you."

I replied, "Fine, because I want to see him too."

She called him and he appeared, looked at me, and in his deep drawl said, "Boy, I want to speak to you."

127

He pointed to his trailer, indicating he wanted me to go there. Inside, I noticed tears again filled his eyes. He pointed to the chair he wanted me to sit in and, just before he opened his mouth, I sensed the Lord wanted me to face him squarely with his need of Christ.

Before he could say anything to me I asked, "Mr. Clay, what is your relationship with Jesus Christ? Do you know him as your Lord and Savior?"

He started to weep like a baby. He sobbed, "Vince, I don't know!" I asked him if he would like to make sure. He replied, "I'd like that fine!" I told him he was going to pray with me, but he said, "I can't pray out loud."

"Yes, you can! Will you pray with me?"

"Yes, I'll try." We bowed our heads and Mr. Clay asked Jesus Christ to come into his heart.

As soon as he received Christ as his Savior, Mr. Clay jumped up, went outside, and called his wife, my wife, and their hired man into the trailer. He told them, "We're going to have a prayer meeting. Reverend, will you pray?" We had a wonderful time of prayer and sharing.

About a month later, I learned Mr. Clay was ill again, and in the hospital. I went to visit him and found his faith strong. The fifth or sixth night, he went to be with his Lord. Mrs. Clay said I was the last person to see her husband alive. I had visited him the night he expired. This was a deeply rewarding experience for me.

I recalled that the night before we were to leave the vacation campsite, I could not sleep. The burden of the man's soul was upon my heart and until about four in the morning, I read the Bible and prayed for him. And God prepared Mr. Clay's heart to receive Jesus Christ as his Lord and Savior! One of my minister friends, Peter Slagle, said of this experience, "Vince, this is called a divine appointment."

My prayers increased for God to use me to introduce many others to him.

11

A New Ministry

Near the end of September I received another letter from Reverend Smoot, with another invitation for me to go to Florida. I wasn't too keen about going again. As a matter of fact, I didn't want to go. Still I felt something compelling me, almost as though I had nothing to say about it. Between my first and second visits, I kept thinking about my friends who had died from using narcotics. I thought of others in hospitals, their emotional problems due to using heroin and other narcotics, stimulants, and barbiturates. Their faces seemed to come to me at night, just before I went to sleep.

I sensed God was speaking to me, but I still fought it. I didn't want to go to Florida. I didn't want to work with drug addicts. As a defense, I even developed a dislike for Mr. Smoot.

Late one evening I searched the Scriptures concerning my going down to work with drug addicts. In the quiet of my study, I read Romans 15:20-21. Through these words I believe the Holy Spirit spoke to me in a very dynamic way, *Yea, so have I strived to preach the gospel, not where Christ was named, lest I should build upon another man's foundation. But as it is written, to whom he was not spoken of, they shall see, and they that have not heard shall understand.*

I thought of many young people on narcotics who have never heard of the love of Jesus Christ. They hear about everything else. While experts argue about which approach is the right one, drug abusers die. So few people really take the love of God to them.

In my mental struggle I realized it was the love of God that freed me of drug addiction. It was the love of God that made me see I was wrong, that I was living a self-centered life, that I was possessed by heroin. It was Jesus Christ who opened my eyes and gave me the motivation to go back to school. It was the gospel of Jesus Christ that made me realize why I was using narcotics. It was the gospel that revealed to me the insecurities I had, the hatred for my parents, relatives, the law, and phony society.

And I thought that if this same gospel could be brought to these young narcotics users, maybe some of them would come to that turning point, accept Christ, and give up drugs. There in that quiet office, I made a great decision.

I went into the house and told Ruth I thought we would be going to Florida. Giving me that knowing look, she said, "I knew it all the time."

I called together my board: Mr. Fred Geraldson, Miss Harriet Hammond, Mr. Steve Miller, and our secretary, Miss Nancy Oliver. I explained my call to work with drug addicts, telling how, as an ex-user, I would be able to relate to these young people in their own language, to tell them of the love of Jesus Christ. Taking my decision graciously, the board wished me God's blessings.

I flew to Miami for the second visit and there learned Denver Smoot had a schedule for me that sounded like a barnstorming evangelist's schedule. Every day was an eleven- to thirteen-hour day. Some days I spoke three times in three different places. Both Denver and I felt we had never seen the Lord work in such a marvelous way as we did that second week I was in Miami.

Forty-five minutes after I landed at the Miami airport, I was to speak at a church in Coral Gables. During this drug workshop, I was supposed to tell some of my drug experiences. Participating at this workshop were Denver Smoot, young Seadog, Dr. Yates who is a neurosurgeon, and Dr. Stillwell who is a psychiatrist.

We were supposed to have a panel but lack of time caused it to be cut short. We watched a film about what marijuana does to a person's health. After the film, we had a question-and-answer period.

Some of the questions asked of Dr. Yates were directed to me by his saying, "I think Vince is better qualified to answer that question because of his past experience." This startled me and I felt small standing next to him. The reason Dr. Yates didn't answer, I figured, was because he did not know experientially and was willing to admit this in public.

The next night Denver had arranged for me to speak at the Coral Ridge Presbyterian Church. The pastor of that church is Dr. D. James Kennedy. Before the service there was a Men's Fellowship dinner at which I met Dr. Kennedy. In his presence I had the feeling I was in the presence of a man of God. There was a great attendance that night. Many of the people came to hear one of the young converts. After this young person gave his testimony I was asked to give mine.

The Lord seemed to work in a very peculiar way. In my discourse I spoke in a much more humorous vein that I usually use. The group seemed to accept it in the right spirit. I learned after the service that one of the young men, a drug addict, spoke to Glen, one of the directors of the House of Ichthus coffeehouse in Fort Lauderdale. Arnette, the young addict, told Glen my story was like the story of his own life. He said he was ready and willing to get off drugs and accept Christ.

A housewife also called Glen and told him about her drug problem. Apparently no one knew she had been taking barbiturates for a long time. She thought that now she was addicted. However, she never realized she had a problem, until that night.

Following the service, we rushed to a home where some sixty people gathered to hear me. We arrived at Reverend Smoot's home about 1:30 A.M. Was I beat! The next day, Wednesday, I addressed a group of ministers from south Florida. One reason for my meeting with these ministers was to seek financial support. We knew it was going to cost a great deal of money to move my family to Florida, provide salary, housing, and transportation.

I shared with those men how the Lord worked with Ruth and me after I graduated from college, how he had given us a wonderful baby boy. Many of them must have shared my own emotion. Tears came to veteran eyes. The group spontaneously broke into singing with deep feeling, "O, How I Love Jesus." What a rich experience it was for me to have been there that day.

That evening I spoke at the annual business meeting of churches in the south Miami area. I felt that, along with my testimony, the Lord gave me a message to preach to the people attending the meeting. There was warm and positive response to what I said.

Immediately after that meeting I went to speak again at the House of Ichthus coffeehouse in Fort Lauderdale. About one hundred twenty-five young people jammed the coffeehouse that night, due in part I think, to the splendid write-up the Fort Lauderdale newspaper had printed along with my picture.

That night I did something I'd never done before: I preached the gospel in hip talk, the vernacular of the young people. My talk hit mental funnybones, judging by the frequent laughs, but I believe the message struck home. Coffeehouse crowds give one of two responses when they appreciate what is said or done: they applaud with great gusto or they do and say nothing. At the end of my discourse in jive talk there was neither applause nor hiss—only quiet, which indicated that something significant and meaningful had happened. Reports later indicated that four or five young people that night turned to Christ for help. It was my privilege that night to introduce a young lady to the Master.

After I met with the ministers of the south Miami area, the word *turning* kept going through my mind. I kept thinking, searching for a title for this book. And I kept seeing a circle with a door leading into the circle and a person—presumably an addict—going through the door and walking around this circle. He was turning around. As I thought about turning, the word *point* came to me. Suddenly I thought, *The name of my book is to be, The Turning Point!*

I asked Denver if he knew of any organization in Florida with the name of Turning Point. He looked at me for awhile, then said, "This could be the name of our organization: The Turning Point—young people coming to the point of decision and turning to Jesus Christ; parents who misunderstand teen-agers and their drug problems, turning to us for counseling and turning to the Lord for strength.

Thinking there was a great deal of merit in this title, we called Frances Gardner, the author, and asked her what she thought. She said, "I think it's just fabulous! Fabulous!"

We also felt there was need for a rehabilitation center which could be called The Turning Point. Young men needed a rehabilitation center as the turning point in their lives. There they could find compassion, understanding, and, above all, the Lord Jesus Christ. Our thoughts and ideas concerning the Turning Point Rehabilitation Center were like germinating seeds just starting to grow. But we believed God would provide funds and a place to enable us to conduct a vital ministry.

The directors of the Turning Point ministry, Reverend Joe Bellamy, Reverend Peter Slagle, Reverend Denver Smoot, and I spent the afternoon talking about and planning the future of this ministry. I discovered that funds were starting to build up, and we decided there was enough money to move Ruth, Jackie, and me to Florida.

Something else wonderful happened that day. I received a telephone call from a pastor friend, telling of a house for rent. I had hoped to buy rather than rent a house, but pressed for time and money, I asked him about the house. He gave me the address of the landlord.

The next day Denver and I went to see the owner, Mrs. Kelso. She took us into the rental house. I quickly decided it was ideal, just what we wanted. When she heard of the ministry we were involved in, Mrs. Kelso reduced the rental price to a figure within our means. I could hardly believe God was handling details for us so marvelously. From all indications, I felt he wanted me in this drug ministry.

The next day I was scheduled to speak at a private school for boys—three hundred emotionally disturbed young men. Neither insane nor mentally handicapped, they simply had emotional problems. I spoke to those young men, after which we had time for questions and answers. It was amazing how these young people opened up and received Denver and me. One of the teachers came over to us later and remarked, "I have never before seen these boys respond to anyone as they did today."

After the school engagement we hurried to the county prison where I spoke to a number of inmates there, telling very simply what Christ had done for me. We prayed and asked for decisions for Christ. Two young men, one twenty years old and the other nineteen, were very sincere in making their decisions.

I told them, "Simply because you made your decision for Jesus Christ doesn't mean you are going to get off the hook"—I had learned both of them were arrested on marijuana charges. The third man who made a decision for Christ was an Italian from Brooklyn, New York. From what I learned later, this young man became a living witness, along with the other two who accepted Christ. Again, I could only stand amazed in the awareness that God was indeed at work in Miami.

While in Miami I observed Denver Smoot very closely. Reluctantly, I admitted he was a man with great insight and understanding for people. I thought to myself that it might even be a wonderful experience to work with this man full time. The defensive dislike I had had for him melted like an ice cube in the sun as God softened my heart. I began to love and admire Mr. Smoot.

All too soon the week came to a close and I once again jetted away from Miami. But this time I knew I was going back—in the will of God. While making this decision, I questioned whether it was of God or not. Around my wall of doubt crept remembrance of the story of Philip the evangelist in Acts 8. He had been in Samaria witnessing for Christ when God took him away and led him to a lonely man who was hungry for God.

I knew there was a definite place for me to work with drug addicts in Florida. Assured, I knew I had settled the matter. However, my church had to be told, a necessity I dreaded to face.

12

The Turning Point

Once home from Florida I called a meeting of my board of trustees, told them the story and my decision, and submitted my resignation. To my immense relief, they all seemed to understand and accept it. The next Sunday, following my message, I made my announcement to the congregation. It was a sad moment, yet they, too, sensed as I did the working of God. Expressing sorrow over our leaving, they wished us well in doing what they also felt to be God's will for our lives.

After all the people had left the building, I felt good inside. Of course, the burden was much lighter. I went to the altar of the church, knelt in silence and rededicated my life to Christ. I thanked God for the way he had helped the congregation to realize and accept his call upon my life.

Within a few weeks Ruth and I had boxes, bulging with our belongings, stacked almost to the ceiling. Our hearts already were in Florida where drug abusers and others with emotional hang-ups needed a Christian influence. I realized that if I were to go to Florida on my own strength, I would most definitely fail and fall flat on my face. But I was going as a representative of Christ, to do his will and not my own.

Soon after we settled into our house in Hollywood, Florida, many wonderful things began to happen. At a drug rehabilitation session in the county jail, I talked to the inmates about Jesus Christ, telling what he had done in my life. Three inmates made decisions to accept Jesus Christ. One of these was a Spanish fellow named Leo, about forty years old. He said, "Vince, this is the only way out. This has to be the answer. Jesus Christ is the only way out."

In our drug rehabilitation sessions we have many stimulating experiences where kids open up and reveal their inner feelings, the animosity they have for people. As they get their feelings out in the open, we can discuss and talk about them, offering great relief to these young people. Much of our work centers in the House of Ichthus coffeehouse where gather young people who have various needs. Some have difficulty with parents, some have drug hang-ups, some want to get off drugs, some are experimenting with drugs and want to talk about it. Some try to debate the legalization of drugs, a subject I try to avoid since I am no legal expert.

One Saturday night I sat at home. I really didn't want to go to the coffeehouse, but I felt compelled to go. Tired, with two preaching appointments for that next day, I felt only like studying and resting. The compulsion kept pulling me, though, so I jumped up, told Ruth where I was going, changed clothes, and went. But not before I asked her to pray about my going, because I had a strange foreboding.

When I arrived, Barbara and Glen Bondurant, the directors, told me a boy who had recently professed Christ was using drugs inside. I walked in and, looking into his eyes, knew he was high on heroin. He had that telltale dreamy look. We started to talk. I quickly learned this boy had a persecution complex. He figured people didn't like him, and said, "That's why I went back on drugs." Realizing it did little good for me to just sit and listen to him stammer over his words, I prayed with him and left the counseling room.

In the coffeehouse I talked with Glen about the commitments some of the young people there have made. When I said the word "commitment" a young boy standing behind me said, "Commitment to what?"

Turning to him I asked, "Have you never heard of a person making a commitment to Jesus Christ?"

He said, "No." I asked him to step into the counseling room where we could talk without interruption, and I proceeded to share with him about the Lord.

This young boy, Eddie, said, "If there was ever a time I needed God in my life, it's right now." I asked him why and he said, "Because I'm tripping my brain out." He meant he was high on LSD.

I had not had too much experience with kids who used acid so I asked him if he'd like to go for a car ride, thinking it might help. We climbed into my car and drove around. For about ten minutes, I talked to him, trying to keep his mind on reality and life around him.

He paled and said, "You'd better take me to the hospital because I'm getting very sick." I drove back and got Glen since he had more experience with this type of person.

Glen said, "If Eddie wants to go to the hospital, let's get him there in a hurry." At Broward General Hospital, after about an hour and a half, Eddie was given a shot of thorazin to bring him down from his bad trip. I was elected to break the news to Eddie's unsuspecting family.

His father was a construction engineer who, when I told him what had happened, rushed to the hospital upset about his son's being an LSD user.

I told Mr. Fischer, "You'd better calm down. And watch your attitude when you talk to Eddie. If you scare people who are tripping their brains out it can cause mental damage." He walked over to his son and proceeded cautiously to make small conversation. The boy told his father that he was using LSD. I sensed the torn feeling that father had as he listened to his son tell him about his drug use.

While we were in the hospital, Mr. Fischer told me he had given his children everything, including a new car as each child reached the age of sixteen. But one thing was lacking in their lives—the love they should have received from their parents. Materially, they had everything, but there were no inner resources.

The next morning I told Ruth what had happened and she was amazed. On the way to the West Palm Beach church, I said, "Ruth, pray for one person to find Christ in this morning's service." She agreed to be in prayer. When it came time to speak, I shared some of my experiences.

At the invitation, one person came forward. I thanked God, because I had asked him for one soul.

Then two others responded. I mentioned that when I was on drugs and living a sinful life, nobody ever called me a fool, but since I turned to Jesus Christ, many people have called me a fool. I stated that I was glad to be a fool for God.

When I said that, a young man came forward and asked to speak. This young man said, "I know what it is to be a Christian, but I haven't been living up to what I know. I know there are many here who are in the same boat. I'm going to the altar now, won't you join me?" As this fellow left the pulpit to kneel at the altar to renew his covenant with Jesus Christ, I bowed my head and thanked God for honest people like him.

When I raised my head, I saw there were nine or ten people at the altar. After these people prayed and returned to their seats, another group took their places. The entire day was one of great inspiration.

Thursday night at the House of Ichthus was Bible study night. Young Eddie was permitted to attend the study. That night Eddie asked Jesus Christ to come into his heart and he received forgiveness and grace. Then he told Glen that his father had been a minister. When Glen phoned Eddie's mother, Mrs. Fischer started to weep for joy over her son's conversion. We felt this would have a definite bearing on the Fischers' lives. Possibly even, Mr. Fischer might re-enter the ministry, renewing his covenant with Jesus Christ.

Mondays at the Sign of the Fish coffeehouse, Mr. Smoot, Eston Hunter—a drug expert and probation-and-parole officer—and I conduct a drug rehabilitation program. One night, before going to the coffeehouse, I stopped at Mrs. Smoot's house to see how she was, since Reverend Smoot was serving as chaplain on a cruise. She said, "Vince, a young fellow called saying he had just come from Puerto Rico. He wanted Denver. He sounded confused, jumbled his words. He might have been on drugs. He was really upset."

She told me his name was Jimmy Pierce. I casually wrote it on a piece of paper and went on to the coffeehouse. Showing Eston the piece of paper with Jim's name on it, I asked if this fellow had shown up. Eston pointed to a guy sitting across the room. The way he held his stomach and shook with chills while sweat beaded his face, I knew the guy was sick. Jimmy told us he was kicking the habit and needed help. I silently renewed a vow I'd made to myself that I would never take a drug addict into my home either while he was kicking or to just live there, without his being rehabilitated and making a commitment to Jesus Christ.

142

Jim told us about some of his experiences, how he had lived in several South American countries, and smuggled narcotics internationally. He said he was tired of running, tired of shooting dope. Twenty-eight years old, he had made a lot of money but had nothing to show for it.

He said his foster parents were fine Christians. Yet, at the age of thirteen, Jim, along with some friends, held up a bank in a small California town. Caught, he was sent to jail. His story was tragic.

We didn't have any place for Jim to stay so I drove him to Fort Lauderdale, hoping to find Glen Bondurant at home. Around eleven o'clock we reached their house where I explained Jim's predicament. We called up a minister who is also a clinical psychologist. Although he was out of town, his wife, Mrs. Jetter, said we could bring Jim right over.

While Jim stayed there I sat up with him at night and Glen stayed during the day, helping him through his cold turkey ordeal. After two days Jim began to feel better. It took him five days in all to kick, but we still had no place to take him. We didn't want to burden the Jetters, though they told us we could stay as long as was needed.

After several nights with Jim I went home as usual one morning. Ruth was working in the kitchen. I noticed her eyes were puffy so I asked, "What's wrong, honey? You look as though you've been crying."

She said, "I don't know what's wrong, but I have been crying. Last night when I was having my devotions, something happened to me. I had a tremendous spiritual experience. Jesus was so real."

I thought that this was a good time to ask her if I could bring Jim, the ex-heroin user, into our house. I did, and she said yes. I almost dropped when she agreed; as a matter of fact, I surprised myself when I asked her, since she knew I had vowed never to bring one to our home. Untrustworthy as drug users often are, I now felt secure under the protection of God. I knew everything we had belonged to Christ, so if someone stole from us, he'd really be stealing from God.

I told Jim he could stay with us for a few days and he was delighted. He and I had much in common since his life was much like my past life. Jim knew quite a bit about the Bible because of his upbringing by foster parents, but he wanted to know more. He knew very little about making a personal commitment to Jesus Christ, so he and I talked several different times about the meaning of personal decision.

He said he wanted to make a commitment but didn't want to fail, and become hypocritical, telling others he was a Christian, but not living the life. He said, "If I make a decision, I want to be able to live the life and look people in the face."

One morning Jim and I had to go to court, because one of my counselees was to be sentenced. Just before we went to the courthouse I told Jim I was praying for him. I asked if he wanted to make a commitment at that time.

He said, "No, I don't feel that I'm ready for it. I want to think about it more." I didn't push him.

I was getting dressed that night for our Drug Rehab session when Jim came walking into the bedroom. He said, "Hey, Vince, what do I have to do to become a Christian? I want to make a commitment to Christ!"

Standing there half-dressed, I said, "Well, let's pray, Jim. Just repeat what I pray if you really mean it." Jim prayed the prayer of faith and became a Christian.

As this is written he still lives with us. Only God knows the future for him. We're praying that Jim makes it. Jim has gone out to look for a job. And we believe he will find one. Behind him are his high school and some college education—and a dying history of drug-induced horrors. We believe in Jim.

We also believe in hundreds—even thousands— more like Jim, and young Eddie. Persons for whom Christ is a necessary Turning Point for their lives. We pray God's Spirit to lead us into a truly effective turning point ministry.

Date Due